PRACTICAL MORAL AND

POLITICAL ECONOMY

PRACTICAL MORAL

AND

POLITICAL ECONOMY

OR, THE

GOVERNMENT, RELIGION AND INSTITUTIONS

MOST CONDUCIVE TO

INDIVIDUAL HAPPINESS

AND TO

NATIONAL POWER

BY

THOMAS ROWE EDMONDS

[1833]

REPRINTS OF ECONOMIC CLASSICS

AUGUSTUS M. KELLEY · PUBLISHERS
NEW YORK 1969

First Edition 1828

(London: Effingham Wilson, *Royal Exchange*, 1828)

Reprinted 1969 by

AUGUSTUS M. KELLEY · PUBLISHERS

New York   New York   10001

.   .   .   .

S B N   678 00564 8

L C N   68 55706

.   .   .   .

PRACTICAL MORAL

AND

POLITICAL ECONOMY.

PRACTICAL MORAL

AND

POLITICAL ECONOMY;

OR, THE

GOVERNMENT, RELIGION, AND INSTITUTIONS,

MOST CONDUCIVE TO

INDIVIDUAL HAPPINESS

AND TO

NATIONAL POWER.

BY T. R. EDMONDS, A.B.

·· Do unto others as you would they should do unto you."

LONDON:

EFFINGHAM WILSON, ROYAL EXCHANGE.

1828.

CONTENTS.

BOOK I.

ON THE PRINCIPLES WHICH MOST AFFECT THE
PHYSICAL CONDITION OF MAN.

BOOK II.

ON THE POLITICAL RELATIONS OF MAN.

CONTENTS.

PREFACE.

———◆———

THE work comprised in the following pages, is of a character totally different from any work hitherto published. The subjects submitted to the consideration of the reader, are of the most momentous concern to every human inhabitant of the globe. Even if the general conclusions deduced were erroneous, this volume can hardly fail to be highly beneficial to mankind, by turning their attention to those things which alone are deserving of attention. But if the conclusions are connected with the facts by a force little inferior to mathematical demonstration, then will this work be productive of incalculable advantages to the whole human race, by pointing out to them the true sources of power and happiness. I have endeavoured to bring down the most important general truths to the level of the commonest understandings. No previous acquaintance with books is required,—nothing more is required of the reader, than an ordinary degree of attention to the facts or phenomena daily occurring in the world. In many cases, I have not descended to the minute developement and limitation of general truths; because I have felt no inclination to anticipate and obviate the cavils of prejudiced persons, at the expense of the patience of the ingenious and impartial reader. I entertain all due respect for the luxurious beauties and technical accuracies of language; but I do not consider a work of this description a proper place for the display of such beauties or niceties. The truths contained are too important to be delivered in any other than the plainest and simplest language. My object has been, the conveyance of my sentiments by means of such a simplicity and clearness of expression as cannot fail to render them intelligible to all classes of readers. I have favoured no particular party in morals or in politics; on the contrary, every party will find something in confirmation, and something in refutation of its opinions or prejudices.

PRACTICAL

MORAL AND POLITICAL ECONOMY.

BOOK THE FIRST.

ON THE PRINCIPLES WHICH MOST AFFECT THE PHYSICAL CONDITION OF MAN.

CHAPTER I.

On the Necessaries of Life.

IF a comparison be instituted between the human race and other races of animals, the most striking general distinction observed will be the absence in man of that hair or other covering of the skin which is common to all other animals having the same kind of skin. Without a covering of some sort for this naked skin, no animals are capable of a continued healthy existence, not even in the most favoured regions of our globe. But though the human race be the only one subject to the privation of one of the richest gifts of nature, yet a bountiful Providence has bestowed on man such superior powers and faculties, that he is enabled to attain, even in a greater degree, those advantages which a natural hair covering confers on inferior animals.

The chief end for which the skins of brutes are covered with hair, is the protection of their bodies from the effects of sudden alterations of temperature. Every brute is constantly exposed to these sudden or rapid changes of temperature; it is exposed to the vicissitudes of day and night, summer and winter; it is exposed also to the variations of temperature occasioned by being alternately wet and dry, by being alternately in a strong wind and in a calm. By means of the low conducting power of hair, the skin of brutes is maintained at a certain uniform, or nearly uniform temperature.

The first step taken by man in providing a remedy for the nakedness in which nature has left him, is to protect himself from the daily inclemencies, or changes of the weather, by the building of huts or houses of a rude construction. Man has never been found without lodging of some kind. We may conclude, therefore, that *lodging* is a necessary of life to all men, in all regions.

The next step taken by man is to protect himself against the changes of temperature, arising from the alternations of summer and winter. In tropical climates, the mean summer temperature of the atmosphere differs so little from the mean winter temperature, that the naked body easily adapts itself to the change. But in polar, and what are called temperate climates, the difference between the summer and winter temperatures is so great, that the naked human body is incapable of adapting itself to the rapid change. Man provides for these changes, by clothing himself with the skins of animals, or with other materials of low conducting powers. Man, I believe, has never been found without clothing beyond forty degrees from the equator. We may therefore conclude, that *clothing* is a necessary of life to all people living more than forty degrees from the equator.

Man agrees with all other animals in this one respect, that *food* is necessary for his bare existence. Every species of animals appear destined for the consumption of some peculiar kind of food. The natural food of man appears to be the same as that of monkeys—fruits and seeds. But the food of improved man embraces all the animal, and a great part of the vegetable kingdom. Man, in his primitive state, consumed a very small proportion of the whole produce of the earth ; but improved, civilized man, and the brutes which serve him, now consume the far greater part of the earth's productions.

There remains yet another necessary for the secure existence of man. Every species of animals is furnished by nature with the means of defence against the attacks of every other species of animals (flight I include among the means of defence). Savage man is protected from the violence of other animals by the powers residing in his hands, and by a superior share of sagacity. The individuals of every species are, in a state of nature, secure from the violence of one another, by reason of the same weapons of offence being bestowed on all, in an equal degree. But man, in his progress towards perfection, is continually discovering new and improved means of offence and defence. The difference between the means of offence of civilized and savage man is so great, that the latter falls an easy prey to the former. Of two societies, in other respects equally civilized, the existence of the society which has least cultivated the arts of war, is dependent on the will and pleasure of the other society; *national defence* is therefore another necessary of life.

As my readers will be found chiefly beyond the fortieth degree of latitude, I shall take it for granted, *that the necessaries of life consist of food, clothing, lodging, and national defence.* These subjects will be separately considered in the four following chapters.

CHAPTER II.

Food.

THE food of all animals consists either of vegetables or animals, or of both. The stomachs of most animals are adapted to the digestion of one of these kinds only: the stomachs of a small number of species are fitted for the reception of both animal and vegetable food, in which is included the human species. Man may support himself, like beasts of prey, by means of flesh alone. The greater part of the population of our globe derive their subsistence from vegetables, a considerable portion of this population lives on a mixture of vegetables and animals, but a very inconsiderable part of the world live on animals only. It is very difficult to ascertain which of these three modes of subsistence is most conducive to the health and strength of man; because those nations which differ from one another in the article of food, always differ from one another in a variety of other important circumstances. There appear to be sufficient grounds for believing a simple vegetable diet to be superior to a diet compounded of vegetables and animals. The English nation may be taken as an example of people using a mixed diet. The Hindoos and Chinese are examples of people living on a simple vegetable diet : to these may be added the African Indians who live on maize, or Indian corn. There are no grounds for believing the Hindoos and Chinese inferior to the English in health and strength: the African Indians are confessedly stronger than Europeans. Without going so far from home, the Irish people afford us good demonstration, that men living on vegetables only are as strong as men living partly on vegetable and partly on animal food ; for it is well known that an Irishman's day's labour far exceeds that of an Englishman. Although a man's health or strength is not much affected by the kind of food which he is accustomed to consume, yet he cannot suddenly change his food without greatly endangering his health. Sudden changes in physics, and in morals, are equally to be avoided.

With relation to bodily health and strength, it is a matter of little importance whether a nation subsists on flesh or vegetables, or on a mixture of flesh and vegetables : but with relation to happiness, the mode of subsistence is a matter of the greatest moment. The number of people a certain quantity of land will sustain, when producing vegetable food, is ten or twenty times as great as the

number which could be maintained by the same
land employed in pasturing cattle. The strength
of a nation is in general proportional to its population : the nation living on animal food would
therefore fall an easy prey to the bordering agricultural nation, possessing an equal extent of
territory, and the pasturing nation will thus lose
its liberty and happiness. But the designs of
Providence are blindly fulfilled by man ;—men
always act by instinct, never by calculation. No
nation ever increased its population in order to
increase its power. The conversion of a pastoral
into an agricultural nation, was never grounded
on a calculation proving the advantages of such
a change. It is the instinctive desire of having
children which is constantly operating in the
transmutation of pastoral into agricultural nations. Men love rather to change their food than
to be without children : it is a greater pleasure to
them, to live on vegetable and have children, than
to live on flesh and have no children, which is the
alternative presented by nature. Some people are
of opinion, that the habitual eating of flesh is
a great addition to the happiness of man ; but
others, with more reason, think, that an Indian
sits down to his rice with as much pleasure as
an Englishman does to his round of beef—the
one, certain of rising up with reinvigorated pow-

ers and light spirits, the other, having a good prospect of a long hour of heaviness and languor, with the chance of an indigestion.

There are three kinds of food on which man may subsist, viz. flesh, seeds, and roots. As it is manifestly of the greatest importance to know which of these three kinds of food is the best for man, I shall proceed to set before my readers the relations they bear to one another. I intend, in the first place, to show what proportions of nourishment a given quantity of land will yield, according as it produces flesh, seeds, or roots : in the next place, I shall endeavour to show what proportions of nourishment can be raised by a given quantity of labour, according as it is bestowed on the production of cattle, seeds, or roots. To obtain a precise knowledge of the quantity of each kind of food which is requisite to maintain a single man, or a certain population, in good health, experiments must be undertaken on a large scale. To obtain a knowledge of the average produce of a given quantity of land and of a given quantity of labour in a country such as England, there must be a general national return of all the lands in culture, of their produce, and of the labour expended on them. In the absence of such experiments and such returns, we must trust to the observation of individuals for an approximation to

these averages. However, the result of the observations of individuals will serve all useful purposes
nearly as well as the results of the most correct
national returns. There does not exist any great
difference of opinion, among men best acquainted
with the subjects, respecting the above-mentioned
averages. The following assumptions, it is expected, will be found midway between the highest
and lowest averages commonly assumed.

I will first assume that two pounds of meat
nourish as much as three pounds of wheat, or four
pounds of barley, or five pounds of oats, or ten
pounds of potatoes. In the next place, I will
assume the average annual produce of an acre of
land to be one hundred and forty pounds of flesh,
or twenty-four bushels of wheat, or thirty-two
bushels of barley, or forty bushels of oats, or two
hundred and fifty bushels of potatoes, (exclusive
of seed); or by weight, the net produce of an
acre of land to be one of the following :—meat
140 lbs.; wheat 1440 lbs.; barley 1600 lbs.; oats
2000 lbs.; potatoes 17,500 lbs.; hence the proportion of people maintained by each acre, will
be :—in meat 70; wheat 480; barley 400; oats
400; potatoes 1750; and since three pounds of
wheat may be regarded as a fair daily allowance
for a full-grown man, the last numbers will represent the number of days such a man can live on an

acre producing these different kinds of food. The last numbers also show, that an acre of wheat, barley, or oats, possesses nearly equal powers of nourishing. We may say, generally, that an acre of land in animal food will sustain a man *seventy days ;* an acre in corn will sustain him *four hundred and twenty days;* and an acre of potatoes *one thousand six hundred and eighty days :* that is, the quantities of nourishment supplied by an acre in cattle, corn, and potatoes, will be as the numbers *one, six,* and *twenty-four,* respectively. In other words, a given territory in corn will maintain *six* times as large a population as the same territory would in pasture ; and a given territory in potatoes will maintain *four* times as. many people as the same territory would in corn.

My next object will be to furnish my readers with a rough estimate of the quantity of labour which is expended on raising and bringing to market the produce of an acre in cattle, flour, or potatoes. We will first assume that land, whether in pasture or in tillage, requires manuring once every two years, and that each acre is manured by twenty cart-loads of dung, drawn by three horses a distance of two miles : it may also be assumed, that each horse requires the attendant labour of one man to drive the cart or spread out the manure. We shall then have, supposing the horses to move at the rate of two miles an hour, for eight hours a day, the labour of three horses and three men for five days to manure an acre for two years ; and for the annual labour of manuring an acre of land, that of three horses and three men for two days and a half, or of *one man and horse* for about *seven days*. If we assume that two horses and two men will plough an acre in two days, and that an acre in tillage requires annually three ploughings, and harrowings and sowing equivalent to two ploughings more, we shall have for the annual labour of tilling an acre of land, two horses and two men for ten days, or one horse and man for twenty days. We will next suppose that the labour required to cut, carry to the barn, and thrash the produce of an acre in corn, is equal to that required to dig and carry to the barn an acre of potatoes ; and we will suppose either of these to amount to the labour of one man and horse for eight days. Again, we will suppose the barn to be distant two miles from the market-town, and that the labour required to grind the corn and carry it to market, is equal to the labour required to transport the greater weight of potatoes to market ; and we will assume this labour as amounting to that of one horse and man for six days. On the foregoing suppositions, the expenditure of labour in bringing to market the produce of an acre of land, in flour or in potatoes, will be equal, and this labour will be that of one horse and man for forty-three days. But the labour required to bring the produce of an acre in cattle to market will amount only to that of one horse and man for seven days. That is to say, the whole labour expended on raising and bringing to market the produce of an acre in flour, or in potatoes, is *six times* as great as the labour expended on bringing to market the produce of an acre in cattle.

I shall now proceed to deduce some important conclusions from the preceding statements. Since the weights of the produce of an acre in meat, flour, and potatoes, are as the numbers *one, ten, and one hundred and twenty*, respectively ; and since the labour required to bring the flour or the potatoes to market is *six times* as great as the labour required to bring the meat to market; the labour required to produce and bring to market one pound of meat, flour, or potatoes, will be nearly as *twenty, two, and one*, respectively. Again, since the powers of nourishment in an acre of cattle, corn, and potatoes, have been shown to be as the numbers *one, six, and twenty-four*, respectively ; and since the labour expended on tilled land is *six* times as great as that on pasture land, we get the labour necessary to provide a given quantity of nourishment in meat, flour, and potatoes, as the numbers *four, four, and one,* respectively.

The above calculations, if expressed in other words, amount to this,—that a given population may be fed by the same quantity of labour, whether bestowed on the production of corn or cattle, but *six* times as much land will be required in the latter as in the former case ; and that a given population may be fed with potatoes, by means of one quarter of the labour, and one quarter of the land, which would be required to feed it on corn. Hence, to a people possessed of a given territory, the national advantages of living on meat, corn, and potatoes, are as the numbers *one, six, ninety-six,* respectively ; this national advantage being properly measured by the ratio compounded of the number of people fed by a given space of land directly, and of the labour expended in the production of a given quantity of nourishment inversely.

We will now suppose, as before, that a grown man would consume three pounds of bread a day, or that, in a population of old and young, the average daily consumption is two pounds of bread, or its equivalent in meat or potatoes, then the labour required for the subsistence of each individual for a year on meat, flour, or potatoes, (being, as before shown, as the numbers *four*

four, and one,) will, for meat or flour, amount
to the labour of a horse and man for twenty
days, and for potatoes, a horse and man for five
days. And if we suppose the population to be divided into families of five persons each, and that one
man provides subsistence for the whole family, this
man must labour *one hundred days* in the year to
sustain his family on *meat* or *corn*, or *twenty-five
days* in the year to supply them with *potatoes*,
supposing him in each case to have the assistance of
a horse. It is necessary to remark, that in order
to estimate the horse's annual labour profitable to
man, we must deduct from the whole labour of
the horse that part which is necessary to sustain
itself and progeny; this part may be assumed
to be forty days, together with a man for forty
days, employed on one acre of land. We shall
then arrive at this general conclusion,—the labour
of one horse and man for three hundred and forty
days, (besides maintaining the stock of horses,) is
sufficient to provide meat or flour for *three* families, or potatoes for *twelve* families, for a year.

Variety is one of the principal sources of the
happiness of man; innumerable modes of cooking
potatoes or other roots may be called into action,
to satiate this passion for variety; and corn and
meat repasts may be indulged in occasionally for
the same reason. What, therefore, is to be re-

commended to a nation as most conducive to its power and happiness, is, to derive its principal sustenance from roots, and for the sake of variety to have corn repasts occurring with tolerable frequency, and meat repasts occurring at long intervals. Fish is manifestly one of the best articles of consumption.

We shall not err far from the truth, if we assume corn or grain to be the food of all nations; for in those countries in which much flesh and roots are consumed, the land and labour which are in excess in providing flesh, may be considered as compensated by the diminished land and labour required to provide potatoes or other roots. My calculations, which apply more particularly to England, may have their application easily extended to most parts of the world, by making allowances for the different states of agriculture, in different countries. Food being the chief article of consumption of all men, and the kind of food consumed being corn, it will be proper to repeat what has been shown above, viz. that in a nation, where the art of agriculture has made any considerable progress, *the labour of one man and horse for three hundred and forty days a year, is sufficient to support with corn fifteen people, or three families, and that each acre will yield corn enough for two people.*

CHAPTER III.

Clothing.

WE have already seen, that a principal distinction between man and other animals consists in his being unprovided with any natural covering ; and it appears to have been the intention of Providence, that man should provide and fashion for himself a covering out of materials with which the world abounds. Every man of reflection must perceive, that the best clothing for man is that which most resembles nature's clothing of other animals. Hair, wool, or down, are therefore to be preferred in clothing to such vegetables, as flax, cotton, or hemp. The functions of the hair covering of animals are, to preserve the body at its proper natural temperature, by means of its low conducting power, to aid the evaporation of any accidental moisture on the skin, and to assist in that part of the animal economy called transpiration. This last function of the hair is apparently of such primary importance, that even man is not destitute of hair on those parts where the perspiration is most copious. None of the above-mentioned functions are found to be performed so well by vegetables (as flax and cotton) as by hair or wool; nevertheless, on account of the facility of obtaining flax, compared with that of obtaining wool, flax is with propriety more generally used for clothing, than wool.

Much more clothing than is necessary is consumed by the civilized world. Custom or fashion compels civilized man to wear much more clothing than is agreeable, much more than is wholesome. I shall, however, consider more than a sufficiency of clothing as necessary. We learn from late French statistical returns, that the average annual consumption of each individual in that kingdom in clothing, is about two pounds of wool, two pounds of flax, and one pound of cotton. We may therefore assume as a fair annual allowance for each individual's clothing in a temperate climate, two pounds of wool, and three pounds of flax, which raw materials we will suppose to be woven into eighteen yards of cloth. The wool of a sheep weighing about eight pounds, and the average produce of an acre of land in flax being six hundred pounds, each individual will consume annually in clothing *one-fourth* of the wool of a sheep, and the *two-hundredth* part of an acre of flax.

I now proceed to estimate the labour necessary to produce the above mentioned clothing. The labour expended on the production of the wool may be neglected, as sheep will probably be reared for their flesh. The labour required to produce the flax, is at the rate of the two-hundredth part of the labour on an acre of land in tillage, for each individual; that is, according to preceding calculations, the labour of a horse and man for *three* days a year, is sufficient to supply with raw flax three families, or fifteen people.

The manufacture of the raw materials into cloth will be performed by machinery, and the moving power will be either steam or animals. If the power of animals be employed, it may probably be fairly assumed, that the labour of a horse and man, for seven days, is sufficient to manufacture seventy-five pounds of raw material into two hundred and seventy yards of cloth, (which quantity we have supposed requisite for the clothing of fifteen people.) If steam be used, a much smaller quantity of labour will be required for this purpose. The labour of manufacturing would then amount to very little more than the labour necessary to dig and transport the coals; for since a steam-engine lasts a great number of years, the whole labour of constructing and repairing the engine must be divided among a very great number of days; and this fraction of labour is evidently inconsiderable when compared with the daily labour expended on obtaining coal.

We may then fairly conclude, that *the labour of a horse and man for ten days*, is sufficient to produce and manufacture cloth enough for the comfortable clothing of *three families, or fifteen people*, for a year.

CHAPTER IV.

Lodging.

THE next necessary of life we have to consider is lodging, under which term I would wish the cooking or dressing of food to be comprehended. As in the preceding chapters I have treated of plain food and plain clothing, so in the present chapter I intend to treat of plain lodging only. The plan of lodging which I am about to propose is not founded on the distinction of people into families; at least, not of families united by the ties of relationship. Some of my readers may be of opinion that the division of people into small societies, united by the ties of friendship, may not tend to increase the general stock of happiness; I must refer them to a future chapter for answers to their objections. I shall content myself, for the present, with assuring them, that nine-tenths of the ordinary labour expended on lodging may be saved by the division of people into families, of which a similarity of opinion or friendship is the bond of union.

I begin by assuming, that a room twenty feet by twenty feet, and ten feet high, would be a wholesome sleeping apartment for eight grown persons, or for ten people of different ages. Then a building of three floors, one hundred and twenty yards long, fifteen yards wide, and twelve yards high, would contain commodious sleeping apartments for one thousand people; each individual having forty square feet of flooring. Seeking the dimensions of a dining-hall for the same number of people, we will assume that a space of six square feet is sufficient dining room for each individual. Then a room containing six thousand square feet, or a room forty feet by one hundred and fifty feet, will be sufficient for the dining together of one thousand people. If this dining-hall be about twenty-two feet high, it would occupy one-third of a building equal in size to that we have supposed appropriated for sleeping in. If we suppose the remaining two-thirds of such a building to be set apart for libraries, lecture-rooms, exercise-rooms, kitchens, &c.; in that case, two buildings of the size above-mentioned would suffice for the comfortable accommodation of one thousand people.

The houses being built, the next step is to furnish them, and warm them in winter. The furniture, being very plain, would cost very little labour in the production. The furniture of the sleeping apartments might consist of a bedstead, feather bed, three blankets, and two sheets for every two people. The furniture of the dining-hall would consist only of tables and benches. The labour required to erect these buildings, and to manufacture the furniture, might be estimated; but as the houses and furniture will last a great number of years, this labour, divided into as many portions as there are years, and again into as many portions as there are people, will manifestly give a very insignificant fraction as the annual contribution of each lodger. It will be found, that (with the exception of about four yards of sheeting) all the labour expended in the production of plain lodging for an individual, resolves itself very nearly into the labour expended on the production of the coals necessary to dress his food, and to warm him in winter. I shall now endeavour to approximate to this necessary quantity of coals.

It is probable that ten or even twenty times as much coals as is necessary is consumed in the ordinary method of warming rooms, and dressing food in England. The most economical method of warming apartments is, either by the distribution of heated air, or the conveyance of steam : the most economical mode of cooking is by means of steam of a high temperature. The precise quantity of coals necessary to warm an apartment of a given size, and to dress a given quantity of food, might be ascertained by experiment; but as we have not these experiments, we must content ourselves with a general approximation. One pound of coals will raise the temperature of one cubic foot of water 150° of Fahrenheit, and four thousand cubic feet of air 20° of the same thermometer. It may be supposed that the difference between the temperatures of the internal and the exterior air is generally 20°; it may also be supposed that the caloric evolved by one pound of coals is sufficient to make good the absorption of caloric during the space of one hour, by the walls and by the ventilation of an apartment containing four thousand cubic feet of air, (at the above difference of temperatures.) On these suppositions, it will be found, that either of the buildings we have mentioned, containing four hundred thousand cubic feet, will require one hundred pounds of coals to warm them for one hour. If we suppose fires to be required six months of the year, and for fifteen hours a day, then eighteen bushels a day, or ninety chaldrons of coals a year, will be required for the warming of one thousand people. One additional bushel of coals a day may be considered enough to dress by steam food for the same number of people, (the caloric used in cooking being afterwards used in warming the rooms). That is to say, one hundred chaldrons of coals are sufficient to warm the apartments and dress the food of one thousand people; that is at the rate of thirty-six bushels each individual for a year.

If we suppose the labour of producing four yards of sheeting to be equal to that required to produce fourteen bushels of coals, we shall have the annual labour expended on lodging each individual, equivalent to the labour expended on the production of five bushels of coals. Consequently, the lodging of fifteen people will cost as much labour as seventy-five bushels, or about two chaldrons of coals. Now the labour of a man and horse for five days may be considered as fully sufficient to dig, raise, and transport two chaldrons of coals.

We conclude then, that *the labour of a man and horse for five days* every year is sufficient to *lodge* comfortably *fifteen people, or three families.*

CHAPTER V.

Military and Naval Defence.

THE three last chapters have been devoted to the consideration of the three necessaries of life, food, clothing, and lodging, which are inseparably connected by nature with the constitution of man. There remains yet a necessary, which, though not established as such immediately by nature, will nevertheless continue to be an important necessary as long as the human race is divided into nations, and those nations into orders and ranks. Military and naval defence will continue to be a necessary until the whole of the human race have nearly reached the limits of perfection in the arts and sciences. National forces are indispensable for the secure enjoyment of the other necessaries of life : without an army and navy, the produce of a nation's labour would lie at the mercy of foreign troops.

It may be assumed that a population of twenty millions requires a standing force of one hundred thousand soldiers, and twenty-five thousand sailors: that is, the standing forces of a nation should constitute the *hundred and sixtieth part* of the entire population, or the thirty-second part of the population of the military age and sex.

The maintenance of an efficient army resolves itself into the labour expended on the production of food, clothing, and lodging for the soldiers, on the manufacture of arms and ammunition, and on the sea or land carriage of stores. The maintenance of an efficient navy resolves itself into the labour necessary to fell and transport timber to the dock-yards, and to construct, equip, and provision the ships.

In order to obtain an approximation to the quantity of labour requisite to maintain an ade-quate standing force, we will suppose, that every efficient soldier or sailor costs the nation three times as much labour as would be required to supply him with the ordinary necessaries of life. At the end of this chapter it will be shown that the constant labour of one man and horse is sufficient to supply fifteen people, or ten grown men, with the necessaries of life. Hence, about forty thousand men and horses labouring con-stantly, can maintain, in an efficient state, an army and navy of one hundred and twenty-five thousand men, which is a proper standing force for a po-pulation of twenty millions of people, or of four millions of men of the military age. That is to say, a sufficient national standing force may be maintained by the constant labour of one man out of every hundred of grown men, or by the labour of every man for the hundredth part of the year, or 3.65 days: so that the labour of one man for 10.9 days, which we will call ten days, is sufficient for three families.

We conclude, then, that the *labour of a horse and man for ten days* every year is sufficient to supply *three families, or fifteen people,* with the necessary *national defence* by sea and land.

Recapitulation.—We collect from the preceding chapters,—that the necessaries of life are plain food, clothing, and lodging, together with military and naval defence ;—that all necessaries are the produce or the effect of labour ;—that eight acres and a half of land are sufficient for the subsistence of fifteen people and a horse ;—that three families, or fifteen people, may be supplied with corn by means of the labour of one man, three hundred and forty days every year ;—that the labour of one man for ten days will clothe the same number of people ;—that one man's labour for five days will lodge them ;—and that one man's labour for ten days is sufficient to defend the same people.

We are carried then to this important general conclusion ;—THE CONSTANT LABOUR OF ONE MAN AND HORSE IS SUFFICIENT TO SUPPLY

THREE FAMILIES, OR FIFTEEN PEOPLE, WITH
THE NECESSARIES OF LIFE. This will be found
to be a close approximation to the real state of
things in a nation advanced as far as England in
the useful arts.

CHAPTER VI.

Useful Labour.

ALL useful labour—all labour contributing to
the power of a people, is engaged in the attainment of the subjects discussed in the preceding
chapters, viz.:—plain food, clothing, and lodging,
together with national defence. Wealth properly
consists in the abundance of the above-mentioned
necessaries. Luxuries have frequently been mistaken for wealth, because they are often found
associated with power: a reflecting mind, however, cannot fail to perceive, that luxuries are only
the effect of an abundance of necessaries or real
wealth. The mental labour of agriculturists, che-
mists, machinists, and philosophers, directed towards the improvement of the means of obtaining
these necessaries, is evidently useful labour; for,
by improvements in the useful arts, a given quan-

tity of labour will produce a larger quantity of necessaries.   I will now proceed to enumerate a
few of such useful kinds of labour, as facilitate the
procuring of national necessaries or wealth.

ROADS.—In order that men may reap the full
benefit of the principle termed " the division of
labour," they must be congregated in towns.
When men are collected into towns, they are
placed at a distance from their food ; and the
larger the town, the more remote must the inhabitants be from the fields, from which they derive
their subsistence. To transport food from the country to the town, a road of some kind would probably be soon made : but among a people who had
not yet experienced the advantages of a good road,
it is not improbable that they would long remain
satisfied with a road of a very rude construction.
It would not occur to them, that by expending a
certain quantity of labour on the improvement of
the road, they might greatly diminish the quantity of labour necessary to transport their food
from the country to the town.   A good road is
nothing more nor less than a machine for the
economizing of labour.   We may suppose, by way
of example, that for the supply of a certain town,
one hundred horses are required to be constantly
traversing the neighbouring roads, whilst the
roads are unimproved.   It is not unlikely, that by

improving the roads fifty horses will perform the same work: if, then, ten horses be sufficient to keep these roads in good repair, sixty horses will, by means of the machine called a good road, perform the work of one hundred horses.

CANALS, like roads, are machines for the saving of labour. If a certain large quantity of goods is required to be transported from one place to another in a certain number of years: then, if the labour of constructing a canal, keeping it in repair, and transporting these goods by it, be less than that required to maintain a good road, and horses to draw the same quantity of goods,—in this case a canal is to be preferred to a road.

SHIPPING.—This is by far the most advantageous method of conveying goods, when practicable. The superiority of this mode of transport over that of canals, chiefly consists in the substitution of the moving power of wind for that of horses. The labour of transporting goods by shipping, resolves itself into the labour expended on, preparing the timber, constructing and equipping the ships, and on the maintenance of one man to about every twenty tons. The labour of transporting a given quantity of goods by sea, by canal, and by roads, are probably as the numbers *one, four, and sixteen* respectively.

MINING is a kind of labour very useful to man, at least the mining for iron, coals, copper, and lead. Iron is manifestly of the greatest importance, coals are useful in the scarcity of wood, copper is useful for the preservation of ships, lead for the purposes of war.

Some other kinds of labour might be enumerated, which have the effect of increasing national wealth ; but what has been said will probably be sufficient to make my readers comprehend what is to be understood by " useful labour." It may be proper, however, here to observe, that such *traffic* alone is to be deemed nationally useful, or conducive to wealth or power, as is concerned in the transport of the necessaries of life, and of the instruments whereby they may be best attained.

CHAPTER VII.

Luxuries.

IT will now be proper to offer a few remarks on the luxuries of life, after what I have stated concerning the necessaries of life. Luxuries, like necessaries, are the produce or effect of labour. Luxuries may be considered to be of two kinds, public and private. Amongst the public luxuries may be reckoned the produce of the labour of the poet, the novelist, the artist, and the dramatist, together with the performance of public singers, dancers, and players. Since the labour of a few men on such subjects is sufficient to produce a great deal of pleasure to a multitude of people, these are luxuries most deserving of public encouragement. Moreover, it ought not to be overlooked, that the labour of producing these luxuries is very frequently a pleasure.

Private luxuries, or the luxuries of individuals, are by no means deserving of encouragement; they should rather be discouraged and repressed. For private luxuries add to the happiness of nobody; but they undoubtedly diminish greatly the happiness of the majority of the human race. Private luxuries consist in the relief from all necessary labour, in the services of domestics, in fine clothes, houses, and furniture; in coaches, wines, jewellery, &c. I have already shown that on the supposition of an equal division of labour, every man would be required to work the third part of the year, or the third part of every day, in order to supply his family with the necessaries of life. If, therefore, a man is relieved from the necessity of labouring, some other must have his portion of labour increased as much as the first man's labour is diminished. If a man,

besides getting the necessaries of life without labour, gets also domestic services, fine clothes, furniture, &c., some other man must have his daily
portion of labour still farther increased.   If there
is any truth in the sayings of the poets and philosophers of all ages, these private luxuries never
contributed to the happiness of a single individual.

If a man, by means of the whip, sword, or money, can command the necessaries, and consequently the labour of ten families, he will naturally employ them in the gratifications of his appetites.   If he lives in a country where the arts
have made little progress, he will retain them
about his person in the capacity of domestic servants.   If he lives in a nation tolerably advanced
in the arts, he will have his appetites most gratified, by retaining only three or four of the ten as
domestics, and by transferring his command over
the remainder to agents, who may return to him
the greater part of the produce of their labour, in
the shape of fine clothes, equipage, wines, &c.   In
order that such a man may be living in luxury, ten
men and their families must be incessantly toiling.

The condition of the day-labourer has frequently
been compared with that of the rich man wallow-
ing in luxuries, with relation to happiness: and
it is often said, that the day-labourer is happier

than the rich man. This is true, in very many instances; because too much labour, and too little labour, are equally detrimental to human happiness. But, generally, the lot of a rich man is better than that of the labourer : for there are ten thousand objects to excite the envy, and cause the unhappiness of a poor man ; he is constantly tormented by the dread of poverty and semi-starvation for his family; and he is capable of few or no mental pleasures and gratifications. This debasement of the mind of man, this degradation of man nearly to a level with the brutes, is what renders private luxuries so extremely pernicious.

Such luxuries have generally been food for taxation, and that very properly : a strong government need never fear a dearth of public labourers, when so many labourers are seen toiling in the production of luxuries for individuals. This government has only to divert the labour engaged in the manufacture of fine clothes, furniture, equipage, &c., into a new channel, wherein the labour of maintaining armies and navies is engaged.

CHAPTER VIII.

Labour and Exercise.

MAN, like most other animals, appears from his constitution to be designed by the Creator to lead a life of bodily activity. His food, the chief necessary of life, whether the produce of the chace or of agriculture, is always the effect of labour. Men who are not, by their circumstances, compelled to daily labour, are universally disposed to undergo some kind of labour, which is then usually denominated exercise. This instinctive desire of bodily motion, is manifestly founded on the constitution of man. Transpiration, secretion, and other functions of the animal economy are but imperfectly performed by a body constantly at rest : it is on the proper performance of these functions that good health depends. Indolence or inactivity of body, besides producing a delicate state of health, frequently causes a sluggishness of the spirits, or a want of vivacity, which is generally productive of unhappiness or misery. Labour or exercise, then, is a necessary ingredient in the happiness of man : I now proceed to enquire what quantity of labour is most conducive to the happiness and well-being of man.

Those men who are in training for the performance of feats of strength, are usually exercised at running for two hours a-day : during the rest of the day they are subjected to some gentler exercise, which may be deemed equivalent to two hours of hard labour; so that we may conclude, in a general way, that a man will enjoy the most robust health, if he be accustomed daily to undergo hard labour or exercise for four hours. But as so much labour might be found painful, and as a smaller quantity will suffice to maintain a good stock of health, so much labour is not generally to be recommended. It is probable that easy walking for four hours a-day, which is equivalent to about *two hours of hard labour,* is the quantity of exercise which would most benefit man.

Our next object of inquiry will be the number of hours per day a master must make a slave or labourer work hard, in order that he may reap the greatest profit from the slave's labour for life. It will readily be granted that a man, as well as a horse, may, by excessive labour, have his strength so diminished, and his life so much shortened, that the total effect of his labour will be much less than it would have been if he had been moderately worked. A horse, if his daily task is too great, will gradually lose his strength, and the animal machine will soon be worn out. If we suppose that a horse thus overworked will

last five years, and that moderately worked he
would last ten years ; and if we suppose that the
effect of the moderate daily labour of a horse is to
that of excessive labour as four to five ; then the
total effect of a moderately worked horse will be
to that of an excessively worked horse, as forty to
twenty-five. But as the moderately worked horse
will last five years longer than the other, the useful effects will be as the numbers thirty and
twenty, or as *three and two*, respectively (taking
the maintenance, or wages of a horse, to amount
to the tenth part of the labour of a moderately
worked horse). Such calculations do not admit
of much precision : the principle is undoubtedly
correct, and the above calculations may be considered merely as an illustration of the principle.
As the laws which regulate the powers of labour
in a horse, are probably similar to the like laws in
man, what has just been stated, may be considered applicable to man. Those who are best
acquainted with such matters, are of opinion that
a horse, to' be most useful, ought never to work
hard more than six hours a-day. It is also
known, that if a horse be worked hard before he
has attained his full growth, the useful effect of
his labour will be considerably less than it would
have been, had he been allowed first to reach his
full strength. From the preceding statements,

we may draw the following conclusions respecting
men :—a slave, or labourer, ought not to be set at
hard work before he has attained his full strength
(say about nineteen years of age) ; and at any hard
labour he must not work above six hours a day,
in order that during his life he may produce the
greatest useful effect for his master.

It has been shown, that, on the supposition of an
equal division of labour (the people living on corn,)
every man would be required to labour for his
family one-third of the year, or the third part of
every day, that is, two hours a-day ; which amount
of labour exactly agrees with the quantity of exercise we have considered necessary to preserve a
man in good health.   The rich would lose nothing
by exchanging their voluntary exercise for some
settled useful manual occupation ; on the contrary,
the rich would be gainers by the exchange, for
they would be then compelled.to take as much
exercise as their bodily health requires, this exercise, when voluntary, being frequently omitted by
an indolent man on any trifling pretence : moreover, it is a common and just remark, that a fixed
easy occupation tends very materially to increase
the tranquillity and happiness of a man.

The greater portion of women in civilized
countries are exempted from hard labour.   The
division of people into families sufficiently ac-

counts for this circumstance, for it requires nearly the constant labour of one woman to prepare the food, and keep the house of one family in order; but nearly the whole of this labour might be saved, if men would alter their mode of living, and form larger families or societies. Women might then divide the hard labour with the men, and take a part proportioned to their strength, in the support of the state. Among most animals, the females have generally two thirds of the strength of the males : a woman will perform two thirds of the work of a man ; but as the woman will not consume more than two-thirds of the food a man will consume, the state is nearly equally benefited by either's labour.

Children also of both sexes, might contribute to the general stock of labour. It probably would not be advisable for their education to cease before the age of nineteen. Until the age of nine, they had better not labour at all : from nine to nineteen, they might with safety be made to contribute labour sufficient to meet the greater portion of the expense of their maintenance and education. If the labour of children be less than that of men, they also consume less than men. The strength of most animals is, for the most part, proportional to the food they require.

In some of the preceding calculations I have

considered the annual labour of a horse or man, as being made up of the labour of three hundred and sixty-five days. I neglect the consideration of the interspersed days of rest, because they exert little or no influence on the total annual effect. The annual effect of the labour of a horse or man would probably be less, if he worked seven days instead of six days a-week.

CHAPTER IX.

Population.

MOST reflecting men will have remarked, that Providence has solidly insured the continued existence of every species, both in the animal and vegetable kingdoms. The principal means whereby Nature attains this object, is the implanting in all animals and vegetables the property of producing many substances similar to themselves. There are very few vegetables which produce less than thirty-fold per annum ; so that in a few centuries, one seed of almost any species of vegetable, might, with its produce, be made to cover the whole earth. Not many kinds of animals increase with the rapidity of vegetables.

The general law of nature which governs the

rate of increase in animals (and probably in vegetables also) appears to be this;—the powers of reproduction in the different kinds, are proportional to the abundance in which the food of each respective kind is supplied spontaneously by a given space of land or water. For instance, a given space of land will produce food for a million times as many insects as quadrupeds ; consequently their powers of reproduction are a million times as great. Again, a given space of land will nourish a thousand times as many rabbits as horses; their powers of reproduction are therefore in that proportion. Again, a given space of land will produce, spontaneously, food for five times as many horses as monkeys, or men in the lowest stage of barbarism ; since the one lives on herbs, the others on fruits and seeds; the powers of increase therefore in horses and men, are as the numbers five and one respectively. The rate of increase of carnivorous animals is an exception to this general law, on account of the difficulty with which their food is procured : carnivorous animals generally increase as fast as herbiverous animals of the same size. It is impossible to ascertain the precise rate of increase in any kind of animals continually changing in their circumstances : we can only expect a rough approximation; but these

approximate rates will suffice for all useful purposes.

My particular object, in this place, is to obtain
a tolerably close approximation to the power of
increase in man, when placed in favourable circumstances. This rate of increase is dependent
on the average duration of man's existence, on
the age of puberty in women, on the average
number of births by women commencing at the
age of puberty, and on the average time intervening between two births. If we take the populations of two countries, and compare them
together in relation to their possible rates of increase, it will be found that these rates of increase
are proportional to the health and strength of the
individuals composing the two populations : a
given number of strong men and women will
increase much more rapidly than the same number of weak men and women. The health and
strength of a man depends on his being supplied
with a sufficiency of plain food, and on his being
accustomed daily to take two or three hours of
exercise, or wholesome labour. Such a mode of
living not only preserves and improves the health
and strength of the present generations; but it
increases the animal power and force of every
succeeding generation. For it is well known that

all vegetables, by attentive culture, can be indefinitely improved in quality and in power of increase : it is also well known that all cattle may,
by careful management, be indefinitely improved
in health, strength, and prolific powers : and it is
not to be doubted that man is capable of a similar improvement, by the same method which improves other animals.

A contrary mode of treatment produces a contrary effect. The best seed will degenerate in a
bad soil and under negligent culture :—the best
breed of any species of animals will gradually decay in health, vigour, and prolific powers, if improperly managed. In the same manner, the
most vigorous race of men will decay if subjected
to improper treatment : the strength of men will
decay, if they eat too much or too little food, or if
they labour too much or too little. The people
of no nation ever regulated their lives in a manner proper to improve their health and strength ;
every population is divided into two parts, rich
and poor ; the rich eat too much and work too
little ; the poor eat too little and work too much.
The extreme into which the poor fall is much
more injurious to the health and strength of man,
than the extreme into which the rich fall : the
consequence is, that the mortality among the poor
is considerably greater than among the rich.

There is no country in the world where the people exert their full powers of increase. The rich refrain from propagating through fear of losing their luxuries, and the society to which they have been accustomed. The poor of all countries refrain from propagating through dread of wanting the necessaries of life. The multitude of unmarried females in every country, who have passed the age of puberty, prove the non-exertion of the people's full power of increase.

Since, then, there are no people who so regulate their living as to produce the greatest measure of health, strength, and prolific power ; and since people in their ordinary indifferent health and strength never propagate as much as they are able, we must not expect to learn from " Population Returns" the natural rate of increase of man. As no people has ever yet had an opportunity for exerting its full power of increase for any considerable period, the rate of increase, as shown by population reports, must always be less than the free and natural rate of increase of a population. If it be true that the population of the American United States doubles itself every twenty-five years ; it is extremely probable that under more favourable circumstances, a certain population would double itself in less than twenty years. Many persons suspect most national population reports of a tendency to exaggeration ; for that reason, I shall endeavour to arrive at an approximation to the natural rate of increase in man, by appealing to individual experience.

The class of men, in European countries, which lives most naturally, and under the circumstances most favourable for the exhibition of the natural rate of increase in man, is that of small proprietors who cultivate their own farms ; they and their children subject themselves to a light labour which is sufficient to keep them in good and robust health ; and they are well supplied with plain food, clothing, and lodging. A proprietor farmer's wife will seldom be found to have borne less than six children ; and it will generally be found that at least four of these children attain the age of sixty years. If we omit the consideration of the two who die before the age of sixty, that omission will probably be more than sufficient to compensate the error we commit, by supposing that each woman gives birth to four children, as soon as she has arrived at the age of twenty years. Expecting that the truth of these observations will be readily allowed, (it being sufficient to consider females only,) we assume,—that one female at twenty years of age yields two females, and then ceases bearing ; that the two latter females at twenty years of age yield four; and that these again in twenty years more give eight females: then, supposing every female to die at sixty, one female infant, at the end of sixty years, will be replaced by six grown females and eight female infants. But the population will not become fourteen times as great in sixty years; because the grown unproductive females existing at birth of first infant, will enter into the proportion. It will be found, however, on the same supposition, which cannot be considered as too favourable, that the population will thus become eight times as great in sixty years; that is, its period of doubling will be *twenty years*.

Having arrived at such a result by a fair induction, we have no reason to be incredulous of the possibility of the statement put forth in the population report of the American United States, that their population doubles every twenty-five years; still less should we doubt the possibility of the truth of the British report, which makes the population double itself every fifty years. There is, nevertheless, a reason for doubting of the correctness of these reports, which reason is the wide difference between the rates of mortality, as shown by these reports, and as found to exist thirty or forty years ago. The pretended diminished rate of mortality cannot be very satisfactorily accounted for. The corn or real wages of labour have not been increased within the last fifty years, and labourers work as hard now as they ever did ; consequently, there is no reason for believing that the poorer classes live longer now than they used to live. The great profits realized by the insurance companies are not caused by a decrease in the general mortality ; but they arise from calculating the value of a rich man's life from tables founded chiefly on the mortality of labourers ; that is, the mistake lies in supposing, that a man enjoying all the necessaries of life does not live longer than a man scantily supplied with necessaries, and moreover subjected to excessive labour. The only probable way of accounting for the asserted diminished rate of mortality is this ;—that the proportion of the whole population supplied with all the necessaries of life has much increased of late years, and that the proportion of the poor and hard labouring classes has diminished. This is probably the case in some degree, but probably not sufficiently so to account for the pretended greatly diminished rate of mortality.

There are many things relating to population, the knowledge of which is extremely useful : for the showing of these things I shall make use of De Moivre's "Theory of Mortality," and of the "British Population Report of 1821." De Moivre considers, that out of eighty-six born, one dies at the end of every year, until all are extinct. According to this theory, a stationary population of three thousand seven hundred and forty-one will be distributed in the series 86, 85, 84, &c. 3, 2, 1, according to ages. According to the same theory, an increasing population will be represented by the series $1 + 2x + 3x + $ &c. $86x^{85}$, where x represents the ratio of the births of one year to those of the preceding year, and where $2x$ and $86x^{85}$, represent the number in their eighty-fifth and first years, where there is one in his eighty-sixth year. The value of (x) may be found by putting the series $1 + 2x + 3x + $ &c., $86x^{85} = (1 + 2 + 3 +, $ &c. 86) × rate of increase in eighty-six years $= 3741 + 3.327$ (according to British Population Report)$= 12446$. Now sum of series $1 + 2x + 3x + $ &c. to (n) terms

$$= \frac{1 + n\,x^{n+1} - \overline{n+1}x^{n}}{(1-x)^2}\, S =.$$ We hence obtain putting $n = 86$, for the value of $x = 1.02$.

If we wish to know the proportion of such an increasing population above the age of sixteen; in the expression for the sum of (n) terms, we must substitute the above value of (x) and put $(n) = 70$. We shall then find that $S = 6250$, which is just the half of the whole series to 86 terms : which shows the numbers above and below sixteen to be equal. But the report states, that the numbers

above and below sixteen years of age as three
to two; which proportion exists, according to
De Moivre's theory, when a population is stationary. The value we have obtained of (x) sur-
prisingly coincides with the average annual ratio
of increase of births, as shown by the report between the years 1801 and 1820. The baptisms of
females in 1801 were 116,508, in 1820 they
were 167,349, which gives us the annual ratio of
increase, or $x=1.02$.

It is impossible to reconcile the statement in
the "Report" with the conclusions deduced from
De Moivre's observations. The truth is probably
intermediate, and the British population probably
increases at the rate of one per cent. per annum,
or doubles every seventy years, instead of fifty
years, as the report states. De Moivre's theory
of mortality, will probably be found very correct
for the population of old and unimproved countries, but it may not be very applicable to people
who have made great progress in the useful arts.
There is much wanted a new theory of mortality,
founded on extensive observations, for Britain. This
theory might be obtained with little difficulty: a
most correct theory might be formed from an annual
return of all the births, and of the ages of all persons
deceased in Britain. In a few years such a theory
might be formed, as would give results much more
worthy of being relied upon than population re-

ports, founded on the laborious and unscientific mode of counting each individual.

A slowly increasing population of a given number, is manifestly stronger than a rapidly increasing population of the same number: for the proportion of grown people will be greater in the former than in the latter case. It may be assumed that all the population below nineteen years of age, and above fifty-nine years of age, are inefficient, or not able to contribute to the national stock of labour. On this supposition, the British Population Report gives the number of the efficient to the numbers of the non-efficient population as nine to eleven. If we consider the women as non-effective, the British effective male population will be to the rest of the population as nine to thirty-one : that is, the effective male population will form the $4.44th\ part$ of the entire population.

It is of importance to know the relative quantities of food consumed by the efficient and non-efficient parts of the population. The power or strength of a population is nearly proportional to the food consumed by the effective part. A grown man will consume less than the double of the quantity of food required by a growing boy of half his weight; because the food of the boy, in addition to the replacing of the parts of his body dissipated by their proper vessels, must be employed in the

increase of his bulk.   The food consumed by the
man and boy is in a lower ratio than that of the
surfaces of the bodies.   I shall assume the mean of
these two to be the true ratio ; that is, I shall assume the food required by a man or boy to vary
as their heights | $\frac{5}{2}$.   I also assume, that a child
having reached the height of thirty-six inches at
three years old, increases in height two inches annually, until he has attained his full height of sixty-
eight inches.   From these data, and from the British Population Report, it will be found that the
food consumed by the effective is to the food consumed by the non-effective, as three to two (women
being considered as effective).   According to De
Moivre's theory of mortality, in a stationary population, the numbers of the effective and non-
effective are equal ; and the food consumed by
effective is to food consumed by non-effective
part of population, as two to one.   Hence it appears (the strength of a population being proportional to the food consumed by the effective part)
that a stationary population is stronger than equal
population, increasing as the British, in the pro-
portion of $\frac{2}{3}$ to $\frac{3}{5}$, or of ten to nine.   This is the
case on the supposition of the correctness of the
British Report and of De Moivre's theory, which
is not exactly true.   If, as is probable, De Moivre's
rate of mortality be too high for Britain, the last

proportion will be nearer that of *five to four* than of ten to nine.

The British Population Report states that there are 10,433 baptisms of males to 10,000 baptisms of females : that the annual baptisms are the thirty-fifth part, burials the fifty-eighth part, and marriages in number the one hundred and thirty-fourth part, of the entire population. From late French Statistical Returns we learn, that the average number of children brought forth by each woman married below seventeen years of age, is 5.44 :—that the average number of children produced by each woman marrying at twenty-seven years and half is 3.846 :—and that the period of fruitfulness of married women extends over a space of 13.3 years.

The United Kingdom of Britain and Ireland contains seventy-four millions of acres, of which at least sixty-four millions of acres may be considered capable of cultivation. Half an acre (with ordinary cultivation) is sufficient to supply an individual with corn, and one acre is sufficient to maintain a horse ; consequently, the United Kingdom contains land enough for the sustenance of one hundred and twenty millions of people, and four millions of horses. We have therefore no reason to apprehend a real excess of population for many years. There may be an excess of population when compared with the quantity of food provided for it.   It will be the duty of the British Government, for many years, to encourage agriculture, rather than to place checks on the increase of the population.

It may here be observed that, if the chief object of population returns be the ascertaining of the strength of a nation, a great oversight has been committed in neglecting the enumeration of horses. For as an engine of labour, and therefore as a source of national power, a horse is equal to five men.   In England, where there is about one horse to every ten people, or two grown men, the effect of the labour of horses is considerably greater than that of man.

CHAPTER X.

Money.

I HAVE carefully abstained in the preceding chapters from all mention of money, because I regard the obscurity in which treatises on Political Economy are generally involved, as mainly to be attributed to the referring, directly or indirectly, of most things to the artificial and inconstant standard of money. Most political philosophers have perceived that the power of money is merely conventional, and that money of itself can occasion none of the necessaries or luxuries of life. These writers have generally acknowledged *labour* to be the prime agent in the production of wealth or power; they have also acknowledged agricultural labour to be the most useful of all kinds of labour; but, judging from the general style of their works, one would not suspect they had ever admitted the truth of these important principles. I believe that none of my readers will now doubt that labour is the cause of all the necessaries and all the luxuries of life. The only effect of money is to distribute these necessaries and luxuries; and my business now is, to show in what manner this distribution is performed.

Money exists generally in the form of gold, silver, or paper. It is evident that neither of these can of itself supply any of the wants of man: it is only from their conventional power over the commodities of life, that they can ever be of value. Men do not love gold for its own sake, but on account of the command it gives them over the commodities of life. Gold is never useful before it has been spent, or before the possessor has given it in exchange for a necessary or luxury. In all countries where the money system prevails, it is manifest that every man can apply to his own use a quantity of the necessaries and luxuries of life, proportional to the quantity of money he can spend. For instance, a man with an income of 30*l.* a-year, can apply to his own use the tenth part only of the necessaries and luxuries which a man of 300*l.* a-year can apply to his use. We shall obtain a correct notion of the operation of money, if we suppose all the effects of labour, all the necessaries and luxuries of life, consisting of food, clothing, lodging, fine clothes, and furniture, domestic services, &c. to be collected into one general fund, and that a man draws out of this fund, a quantity of commodities proportional to his income. But these incomes are dispensed after a very extraordinary fashion; for the general law is, that the man who contributes least to the production of necessaries and luxuries, enjoys the largest income, whilst the man who contributes most to the common general fund, has the smallest income.

The distribution of these incomes is founded on the institution of private property. The command over the whole national stock of necessaries and luxuries, is vested in a few individuals by the rights of property. If these individuals, which we will call the rich, had always managed their own property, it is probable the money system would never have been invented : for in this case the population would consist only of two classes, rich and poor, or masters and labourers ; and it evidently would be less troublesome to the masters to pay their labourers directly in necessaries, than to establish a common fund of necessaries and luxuries, and give their labourers so many counters, or so much money, as would exchange for the bare necessaries of life. In fact, if the population consist of these two classes only, what is usually called slavery will exist. But in all countries where the money system prevails, the people are divided into three classes ; viz. the rich, the labourers, and the managers of the property of the rich and of the labour of the poor, which managers are generally themselves possessed of property : in other words, such a people may be considered as consisting of three classes, rich, labourers, and traders. The national stock of necessaries and luxuries is committed to the care of the class of traders, who distribute these commodities, by means of certain counters called money. The rule observed by the traders in the distribution of these counters is this : first to give to the labourers who produce these necessaries and luxuries, in exchange for their unceasing labour, so many counters as represent their bare necessaries of life ; and then to divide the remainder among themselves and the rich, by giving to the rich man a number of counters proportional to his property, and by giving to each trader a number of counters proportional to the value of the stock under his management. It will thus frequently happen that whilst the labourer gets only one counter, the trader and the rich man are receiving twelve counters each, and consequently applying to their use twelve times as much of the necessaries and luxuries of life.

The difference between the conditions of a slave and of a labourer under the money system, is very inconsiderable. The motive which impels a free-man to labour is much more violent than the motive impelling a slave: a free-man has to choose between hard labour and starvation for himself and family; a slave has to choose between hard labour and a good whipping: which of these two motives is the most cogent no man can doubt. The master of a slave understands too well his own interest to weaken his slaves by stinting them in their food; but the master of a free-man gives him as little food as possible, because the injury done to the labourer does not fall on himself alone, but on the whole class of masters. There are some respects in which the condition of a free labourer is superior to that of a slave. A free labourer has generally the liberty of changing his master: this liberty distinguishes a slave from a free labourer, as much as an English man-of-war sailor is distinguished from a merchant sailor. Another liberty enjoyed by the free-labourer is,—that of spending his money on what kind of necessaries he pleases: he also enjoys the liberty of depriving himself and family of necessaries in order to provide himself with a few luxuries. The condition of a labourer is superior to that of a slave, because the labourer thinks himself free; and this opinion, however erroneous, has no small influence on the character and on the happiness of a population.

The money system not only lessens the number of disinterested friendships, and consequently diminishes the general stock of happiness, but it sows also the seeds of enmity between man and man; for what is gain to one man is loss to some other man. The receiver and the payer of money stand in the relation of enemies to one another; the one strives to pay as little as he can, the other strives to get as much as he can. The class of traders pay as little money as possible to the other two classes, and frequently have recourse to the most disgraceful expedients to increase their receipts from the other two classes. This class of traders again, is at enmity with itself; for if one baker in a town is getting very much money, the other bakers of the town must be getting very little money; if one lawyer has great practice, other lawyers must have little practice; and if a man spends much money at the grocer's, he will have less money to spend at the baker's. The class of labourers are also enemies one to another, because one man's getting employment frequently throws another out of employment. The interests of the three classes are in direct opposition one to another; and the interests of the individuals composing the classes of traders and labourers are opposed to one another; so that the money system may be said to compel one man to become the enemy of almost every other man. One would imagine, that the invention of money must have proceeded directly from his satanic majesty.

Although the money system is so pernicious, it is not however productive of unmixed evil. The slave system has been succeeded by the money system, and the money system will be succeeded by the social system, one system following the other, perhaps in a necessary order. By means of the money system, the useful arts have advanced ten times more rapidly than they could have done under the slave system. By means of the social system, the useful arts will advance ten times more rapidly than they have done under the money system. The perfection of the money system is the commencement of the social system. The imperfections of the money system are being gradually removed. This gradual removal is in consequence of the important and beneficent law of nature, *that no man or class of men can enjoy any durable happiness by the oppression of other men or classes of men.*

Having so far discussed the nature and general effects of money, I shall now proceed to offer a few observations on the quantity of money, or the number of counters in circulation. I shall suppose that the currency shall consist of gold, paper, or bone counters, all of the same value ;— that no payments, either for goods or services, are made in any other money, as bills of exchange ;—that these counters are issued by one single national bank ;—and that the relations with foreign countries do not affect the value of these counters. It is first necessary to remark that the consumption of commodities by a nation, is as regular and unceasing as the current of a large river. If a nation consume a certain quantity of commodities every year, it consumes the 365th part of that quantity every day, or the 8760th part every hour. The food of a man might easily be distributed to him every day ; but the same is not true of clothing

and lodging.   A man will consume a coat every
year, and a house and furniture every one hundred
years ; but the 365th part of a coat and the
356 × 100dth part of a house, can not be distributed to a man every day, so as to serve him for
clothing and lodging.   Articles of food are con-
sumable by parts ; clothing and lodging must be
consumed as wholes.   The use of a coat for a day,
or of a house for a day, might easily be distributed
to every man daily: nothing more will be required
for such a purpose than a large stock of houses
and coats at the disposal of the distributor.

It may now be supposed, that the command of
all the national food, clothing, and lodging, is vested in one individual or one company of men ;
and that this man or company of men has to distribute these necessaries among the people by
means of counters.   It may also be supposed that
all the people are equal, or that each man receives
the same number of counters.   The first subject to
be considered by the distributing power is, whether
the counters it issues are to be returned every day,
or every week, or every month, or other interval. If
it be decided, that all the counters issued shall
be returned within a day, this object will be easily
attained, by making the number of counters issued
represent the necessaries required by the people
for their daily consumption.   If, for instance, the

population amounts to one million, and if the government, having one million counters, should decide that a counter was equivalent to the necessaries every man daily requires, then one man would pay and receive a counter every day ; and the currency of the country would consist of one million of counters returned daily.

In the next place, suppose the government to determine to issue all its counters, and have them returned weekly instead of daily. There are two ways of effecting this object: one way is, by issuing the same number of counters, and increasing the value of each counter sevenfold, or allowing each counter to represent or be exchanged for seven days' necessaries ; the other way is, by increasing the number of counters sevenfold, and by ordering each counter to retain its ancient value.

What has been said is sufficient to conduct us to these important conclusions :—That the whole currency represents or may be exchanged for, the quantity of commodities consumed by the nation in the time intervening between two successive payments. That if the currency or the number of counters in circulation remain constant, the quantity of necessaries represented by each counter will be proportional to the time intervening between two successive payments ; and that the time between two successive payments remaining unchanged, the quantity of necessaries represented by each counter varies inversely as the number of counters.

In modern societies the class of traders perform the function of my supposed distributing power or government; the effects, however, produced thereby on the value of the counters, in no wise differ from the effects of the system I have supposed existing. The class of traders hold in their possession all the necessaries and luxuries of life; and they are continually exchanging these commodities for counters; or they are paying these counters to labourers for producing these commodities, or to rich men as revenue, for the use of their property. In England the payments to labourers are made weekly; the payments to traders and rich men are made, some monthly, some quarterly, and some annually. If the average period of all payments be half quarterly, and if the daily consumption of the English nation be represented by one million gold counters, called guineas; then, that part of the currency used by consumers, would consist of forty-five millions of guineas, or of paper notes representing guineas. If the average period of all payments were doubled, ninety millions of guineas would be necessary: if the average period were to be shortened one-half, twenty-two millions would be nearly sufficient.

I shall reserve the consideration of the trading currency, and of the relative utility of a paper or gold currency, to a future occasion. I cannot here however help observing, that paper counters are evidently preferable to gold counters, because gold counters cost a great deal of labour.

BOOK THE SECOND.

POLITICAL RELATIONS OF MAN.

CHAPTER I.

Division of Labour.

THERE are two bonds by which men are united and collected into societies : one bond of union is the law of nature called gregariousness or sociality, by which men like many other animals, are impelled to seek the company of each other ; the other bond of union is the principle termed the " Division of Labour," which impels men to associate together, on account of the mutual advantages enjoyed by the saving of labour. Barbarous men are united in societies by the former of these bonds alone ; civilized men are united by both these bonds of society. It is hard to determine which of these two bonds is the stronger, in the existing civilized societies. It may, however, in this part of the work, be taken for granted, that the " division of labour" is the only bond of union of political societies.

The advantages attending the " division of labour," may be supposed to have been discovered in the following manner. On the discovery of agriculture, a society of hunters was probably dissolved, by each man fixing his abode on the spot of land which he cultivated for the subsistence of himself and family. The reason which induced the hunters to abandon their village, and break up their society, would be, that the labour of carrying the corn to their village might be saved, by each man residing on the spot where his corn grew. Each man will then have to labour on the land, and to manufacture his farming implements, his clothing, and his lodging: whilst such a state of things continues, it is manifest that all these arts will remain in the rudest state. But Nature has laid down laws for the perpetual improvement of the human race; and men cannot fail to be constantly adding to their knowledge, of the arts in particular. It will soon happen, that one of these isolated men can make better farming implements than his neighbours, and can also make them more expeditiously. A certain number of his neighbours will agree to cultivate his farm, on condition of his supplying them with farming implements. Mutual advantage will occasion this agreement: the expert maker of farming implements will perceive, that it costs him less labour to make those implements, than to cultivate his farm; and his neighbours will perceive, that it costs them less labour to cultivate his farm, than to make their own farming implements. The expert maker of clothes, and the expert house-builder, will have their farms cultivated for them, on similar conditions, and for the same reasons. The population of a neighbourhood will then be divided into four classes, agriculturists, clothiers, builders, and manufacturers of farming implements; and as each of them now gives his undivided attention to a single object, it will soon happen, that each man's dexterity in his business will have so increased, that an agriculturist can produce a given quantity of food, with one-half the labour it would cost a clothier; and that a clothier can manufacture a given quantity of clothing, with one-half of the labour it would cost an agriculturist. When things have arrived at this state, four men will be able to produce as much necessaries as eight men could before: and consequently the country would become twice as wealthy or powerful. Those men who are not agriculturists will probably collect themselves into a village; the labour of transporting their food to the village, will be compensated by the convenience arising from all the artizans being collected on one spot.

The principle on which these men emerging from barbarism have acted, has been termed the "division of Labour." But although they have acted on this principle, it does not follow that they have discovered this principle. On the contrary, it is more than probable that they will be as ignorant of this principle or general law, as ninety-nine hundredths of a population are, who have carried the division of labour ten times farther than themselves. There are few agricultural nations who have not carried the division of labour as far as we have supposed above : it is extremely probable, however, that they would not have advanced so far without the co-operation of the money system. Not ignorant barbarous men, nor even most civilized men, are capable of comprehending the exchanging of labour for labour. Men require something tangible to aid their comprehension ; men have pretty clear notions of exchanging labour for gold, and gold for food, or some other commodity, but very few men can or do perceive that this is nothing more than the exchanging one effect of labour for another, or the exchanging labour for labour. The people, whom we have been supposing emerging from barbarism, will probably

first have money introduced among them, which
money will represent or command all kinds of
commodities ; these people will not perceive that
they are exerting themselves to save labour, they
will be able to perceive nothing more than that
they are saving money. The result, however,
will be the same as if they had a clear understanding of the principle termed " the division of
labour." Without the invention of the money
system " the division of labour" would have advanced very slowly ; the more perfect the money
system becomes, the more labour becomes divided.
Britain has the best money system, consequently
" the division of labour" is carried farthest there,
and Britain is the most powerful and wealthy
nation in the world.

The object of all useful labour is the attainment of the necessaries of life. The labour engaged in producing the necessaries of life may
be divided into the labour of producing food, the
labour of producing clothing, that of producing
lodging, and that of providing national defence.
These four principal divisions of labour may each
be divided into several subdivisions ; and these
subdivisions again may be divided into many
others. In other words, the labour necessary for
every man's comfortable existence, may be divided into a multitude of simple operations. Now

it is found by experience, that if each man of a certain community confine his whole labour and attention to one of these simple operations, the whole quantity of necessaries produced by that community will be considerably greater than it would have been, had each man's labour been directed sometimes to one simple operation, and sometimes to another.   Experience also shows, that the more simple the operations are in which each man is engaged, the greater is the effect produced by the labour of the whole community. This is as much as to say, the more labour is divided in any community, the more wealthy or powerful does that community become.

The principle of " the division of labour " is resolvable into a principle of human nature, which is termed " the power of habit."   This power of habit is partly a mental and partly a corporeal faculty ; it is a faculty which no man can have failed to experience in his own person.   In learning to write, a man or child, by " the power of habit," becomes able to write ten times as fast as he could when he first began to join letters together ; the musician is able to move his fingers ten times faster than he could when he first began to learn music ; the juggler, by practice or habit, moves his hands with such a velocity as to escape the observation of his spectators ; workmen who make nails, pipes, parts of pins, parts of buttons, or other things, are able to work ten times faster and better than they could when they began to learn their business ; even in the simple operation of digging the ground, a man who is accustomed to the work will perform much more than one who is not.   But to acquire this dexterity in the above-mentioned arts much time must be spent ; the longer the time a man practises any art, the more dexterous and expert will he become ; but the increase of his dexterity will not be very perceptible after he has practised two or three years. It may generally be assumed as true of most of the simple operations into which labour has been or will be divided, that a man, by practising one of these operations for three years, will be able to produce a ten times greater effect than can be produced by an unpractised man, in a given time.   It is proper to observe, that the advantages springing from the " division of labour" are much greater in the manufacturing arts, than in the art of agriculture.   In all operations requiring the exertion of great animal force, (such as digging the ground, sawing timber, walking or running,) a practised man cannot produce more than two or three times the effect produced by an unpractised man.

The astonishing advantages attending the " di-

vision of labour," appear to depend on a principle
of the following nature.   The extreme power or
moving force of a certain muscle of the body may
be represented by a certain number which ex-
presses the weight this muscle is capable of sustaining.   The force exerted by this muscle may
always be represented by a weight (representing
the resistance,) multiplied by the velocity with
which this weight is moved.   By the " power of
habit," the latter product may be rendered equal
to the former number.   For example, suppose the
extreme force of a certain muscle to be represented by 100lbs; and suppose this muscle exerted in
overcoming a resistance represented by a weight
of 50lb.   This muscle unpractised will probably
not be able to move this weight with a greater
velocity than that represented by the number one;
that is, this muscle unpractised, will be able to
exert no more than a force of 50lbs.   But after
two or three years of practice this velocity may
be increased to two; and the power of this muscle will have reached its limit, or 100lb.   If the resistance to be overcome be represented by a weight
of 10 pounds, then the limiting velocity of this
weight will be represented by 10: the man learning to move this weight will pass through all the
degrees of velocity from one to ten.   The muscle
moving the juggler's arm, has no other resistance

to overcome than the weight of the arm; the weight moved by the muscle is very small, consequently the velocity attainable by practice is very great, so that the motion of the arm is as invisible as the motion of a cannon-ball.

The division of labour is progressive: operations of the utmost simplicity, can be discovered only through the medium of operations less simple. One division of labour paves the way for a farther division of labour. By one division of labour a man's attention becomes concentrated, and he views the operation, about which he is employed, in every possible light; the consequence will be, the perception of one or more simpler operations, into which this operation may be divided. These operations may be again subdivided, until operations are discovered of such extreme simplicity, as to be performed by plain machinery. The comparison of plain machines one with another will lead to the invention of complex machines, these machines to machines more complex, and so on, until one machine is capable of producing what was before the result of many simple operations of man.

The chief obstacle to the increase of the number of divisions of labour, is the much vaunted principle of *private or individual competition.* In all towns are to be found several sets of masters and men, exercising the same trade, and having no connexion with each other. There is, however, no room for doubting that if all these masters and men of the same trade were united together, a greater subdivision of labour might be effected, and consequently a greater quantity of commodities be produced by the same number of men. The reason why these men of the same trade or business are not united together, is of the following nature. Every capitalist, every commander, or manager of labour, is allowed to fix what price he pleases on his commodities; and all traders, when unopposed, demand such extravagantly high prices, that the public always find, that any article costs them less money when the manufacturers of that article are distributed among two, three, or more masters, than when all these manufacturing labourers are collected under one master. But although by means of private competition, the money price of an article may be diminished, the labour price or true price is increased, and consequently the national power is diminished. We will suppose by way of illustration, that one capitalist manages all the labourers of a certain trade in a town; and that in order to produce a given effect, he must employ twelve men, to whom he pays as wages twelve pieces of money; we will also suppose he charges the public twenty-four pieces for the work done, or that he takes a profit of cent. per cent. The high

price of this kind of work will induce another
capitalist to embark in the same business: he will
draw away the labourers from the first capitalist
by offering higher wages. When the number of
men employed by each capitalist is about equal,
or when they have tacitly agreed on the minimum
price of an article, or on the minimum rate of
profit, then wages will return to their ordinary
level. In order to produce the effect before produced by twelve men acting together, fourteen
men, acting separately in parties of seven each,
will probably be required; and fourteen pieces of
money must be paid by two capitalists, acting
separately, for an effect which could have been
obtained for twelve pieces by one capitalist, or by
both capitalists acting together. We will suppose
that the two competing capitalists consent to
charge no less than twenty-one pieces of money
for what costs them fourteen pieces, or that they
fix the minimum rate of profit at fifty per cent.
It will then happen, that the work done, or the
commodity which cost the public twenty-four
pieces of money when there was no competition,
will cost the public twenty-one pieces when there
is competition. Since this commodity, which now
costs the public twenty-one pieces, costs the single
capital twelve pieces, and the two equal separate
capitals fourteen pieces; two equal capitals, united

into one, would occasion a profit of seventy-five
per cent., whilst each capital separately, will yield
no more than fifty per cent.

The observations I have just now made fully
prove, that the principle of private competition is
not only injurious to the interests of the public,
but is also inimical to the interests of the single
competitors. Private competition would probably
have now ceased to exist in England, if there had
been no laws directly or indirectly prohibiting the
collecting together of the capitals of many individuals, and managing them as a single one.
When the abrogation of these pernicious restric-
tions has set free all capitals or all the national
labour, the capitals employed in every trade will
gradually increase, and the " division of labour" and
the progress of the arts will be most rapid. The
partiality of most national laws is an obstacle to
the establishment of joint stock companies. A
poor man is frequently punished with death for
stealing a very small sum of money, but a rich
man may plunder and steal from his employers
with impunity, provided that he keeps within the
bounds of moderation. An agent, in the service of
a nation or of a company, who takes a guinea
from the money with which he is intrusted, or
who gets a guinea by sacrificing the interests of
his employers, is deserving of as severe a punish-

ment as a poor man who steals a guinea from a till : they both equally infringe the rights of property.   It might, in some cases, be advisable for the national government to fix the highest rate of profit allowable to be received by a company ; but in most cases, the government cannot do better than allow all companies the most perfect freedom of action.   There is perhaps not a law in any country restricting trade, which has not occasioned a greater evil than the evil for which it was proposed as a remedy.   A wise government will endeavour to give the greatest possible freedom and security to property.   Things do not improve under favour of the numerous laws on trade, but *in spite* of them.

I have been using the words capitalist and capital : I shall endeavour to explain to my readers the signification which I wish to be attached to these terms.   I would define a capitalist to be a man who commands or manages the labour which is engaged in the production of necessaries or national wealth.   I have excluded from my definition the labour expended on luxuries, because there is no distinction worthy of notice between the labour of the menial servants of a lord and the labour of men in a lace manufactory.   A capitalist, for the production of necessaries, requires men to labour for him, materials for the men to work up

(called stock), and machines to increase the effect
of their labour; now the materials are the result
or the effect of past labour, the machines used are
the effect of past labour, (but present labour is
generally required to keep the machines in order.)
The materials used, as well as the small machines, are generally the property of the capitalist; but powerful machines, such as improved
land, canals, roads, and ships, are generally the
property of others, to whom the capitalist pays a
revenue for permission to make use of them.   A
capitalist may be said to be the commander and
manager of current labour, enjoying the use of
fixed labour.   I would define capital as consisting
of useful, current, and fixed labour; but, agreeably
to the common acceptation of the term, I do not call
a man a capitalist who does not manage his capital.
The current useful labour of England amounts,
as I have shown, to about that of the third
part of the population; the remaining two-thirds
of the population are employed in the consumption of the wealth or necessaries produced by the
useful labour.   This useful current labour, and
the fixed labour used by it, are alone to be regarded as capital, or as something whence national
wealth or power is derived.   The amount of fixed
useful labour in England is not easily to be ascertained; the chief part of it consists of improved

lands : it probably does not amount to more than the annual current useful labour, repeated four or five times.

The well-known fact that a large capital always yields a higher rate of profit, than a small capital employed in the same trade, does not depend wholly on the division of labour. It would be so dependent, as I have already shown, if the capitalist were the commander of present or current labour only ; but most capitalists have the command or management of passed labour or fixed labour, and some capitalists enjoy the use of much more fixed labour, or more powerful machinery, than others. A machine which costs twice as much as another machine, generally produces more than twice the effect. The " division of labour" occasions the invention and improvement of machinery, and the current labour bears a very considerable proportion to the fixed labour employed by a capitalist; so that the fact of a large capital producing goods at a cheaper rate than a small one, depends in a great measure on the principle of the " division of labour."

Another subject, which may with propriety be classed under the head of this chapter, is the method pursued by men in cooking their victuals. A certain number of men acting separately, would, if collected together, cook the food of ten times as many people as they could before, with the same quantity of coals. In other words, by cooking many persons' food in one place, nine-tenths of the customary labour in cooking and producing coals might be saved.

CHAPTER II.

Commerce.

COMMERCE is founded on the " division of labour." All useful commerce, all commerce occasioning wealth or power, is founded on the reciprocal advantages which attend a division of the labour engaged in producing the necessaries of life. If every man produced his own food, clothing, and lodging, that is, if there were no division of labour, there could be no commerce. Every man must at all times be consuming the three great necessaries of life ; if a man apply his labour to the production of one of these necessaries only, he must exchange part of the produce of his labour for the other two necessaries. As the division of labour increases, the number of exchangeable articles increases, and commerce increases.

The distance of places between which useful commercial relations may exist, is very worthy of consideration. It frequently happens, that a certain commodity can be produced at one place, and then transported a distance of three hundred miles, at the expense of less labour than would be required to manufacture it at another place, and transport it only ten miles. This arises from the relative amount of capitals; I understand capital as consisting of the current labour, and the labour fixed in machines employed in the production of necessaries. Large capitals, or large collections of labour, effect much more, and occasion greater improvements in the application of labour, than they would do if divided into many small capitals. A large capital undersells a small capital, from being, at first, more than proportionally powerful; and afterwards, from increasing more rapidly in power, by means of new inventions. All capitals engaged in the same trade over a large district, have a natural tendency to unite themselves together in one place. When these capitals become so united, they are not again easily separable into small capitals, although such a separation may be very desirable. A union of all capitals engaged in the same art, is undoubtedly most conducive to the progress or improvement of that art: but when an art has nearly reached perfection, it is generally more profitable to have the whole capital employed, spread in smaller portions over a country. When capitals are very large, the produce of these capitals must be transported to a great distance ; when capitals are small, commodities are consumed where they are produced. In England, the capitals employed in the manufacture of clothing, are, for the most part, collected into one small district : consequently, the labour required to transport clothing to the consumers, and food to the manufacturers, must be very great. It is not improbable, that the whole labour of producing and transporting clothing, would be diminished by dividing the capital employed in the manufacture of clothing into several small capitals, at the distance of about fifty or sixty miles from each other. But it is no easy matter to transport capital from one part of a country to another: in the first place, the workmen and their families are to be conveyed ; in the next place, the moveable machinery is to be conveyed; but with respect to the fixed machinery or capital, it cannot be conveyed away at all. A large capital employed in any branch of manufactures, is so much dependent on other capitals, in different branches of manufacture, that one capital cannot be advantageously removed, unaccompanied by several other capitals. If the agricultural population of each district were to attempt to create for themselves a manufacturing capital, they would have to commence at the first step in the progress of the division of labour; they would advance no faster in the manufacturing arts than agricultural nations generally do ; and their manufactures would cost them much more labour than they might have obtained them for by exchanging corn for manufactures.   The manufacturing districts of England bear the same relation to the rest of the world, (which is chiefly agricultural,) as they do to the agricultural population of England. The English agricultural population, if they attempted to produce their own clothing, would find that it cost much more labour than the corn which they were accustomed to give the manufacturers for it: similarly, the French nation would find, that they could grow corn, carry it to England, and receive a certain quantity of manufactures in exchange, at a less expense of labour, than the direct production of the same quantity of manufactures would cost in France.   The natural difficulties of transferring capitals from one district of England to another, and from England to France, are of the same character.

Before the ' division of labour,' every man produced his own food, clothing, and lodging, and the machines or tools he wanted.   On the discovery of the properties of iron, it is probable that labour was first divided ; the first division of men was probably into these two classes, viz. the producers of the necessaries of life, and the workers in iron, who produced the requisite machines or tools. The first commerce consisted in the interchange of iron machines for necessaries : those who lived near the workers in iron, would give corn in exchange for their iron tools ; those who lived at a distance would give clothing in exchange for their iron, in order to save labour in carriage ; since the weight of a certain quantity of clothing will not be greater than the tenth part of the weight of a quantity of corn of the same value. When the labour of producing corn and clothing becomes divided, commerce will consist in the interchange of corn, clothing, and machines : every grower or producer of corn alone, must give part of his corn for clothes and machines ; every producer of clothing alone, must be continually exchanging part of his produce for corn and machines ; and every machine-maker must be exchanging part of the effects of his labour for part of the effects of the labour of the corn grower and the clothier. All useful commerce consists, almost wholly, in the interchange of these articles,—corn, clothing, and machines. All other commerce produces no more national wealth than does the labour of domestic servants. Since the consumption of tools or machines is not

considerable, when compared with the consumption
of either corn or clothing, it will be sufficient to
consider all useful commerce as consisting in the
interchange of corn and plain clothing.

When a population has divided itself into
clothiers and agriculturists, the produce of the labour of the entire population soon increases. The
agriculturists having their attention confined to
one subject, will divide their labour, and soon discover improved methods of applying their labour;
so that it is not improbable, that at the end of one
hundred years, the labour of one agriculturist can
produce twice as much corn as it would at the
beginning of that time. The effect of the labour
of the clothiers will increase much more rapidly,
because the art of making clothing may be divided into many more simple operations than the
art of producing corn. At the end of a hundred
years, the effect of the labour of one clothier will
probably have increased tenfold. On these suppositions, a certain quantity of corn will exchange
for five times as much clothing as it did one hundred years before; for it may be taken for
granted, that things which cost the same labour,
are of nearly equal value in exchange. If it be
supposed, that at first the proportion of agriculturists to clothiers was that of three to one; at
the end of a hundred years, the effect of a given

quantity of labour in cloth and corn together will
be quadrupled. But on account of the labour
saved on cloth being applied to agriculture, the
power of the population will only be a little more
than doubled in a hundred years; at the end of
which time, the agriculturists will be to the
clothiers, as fifteen to one.

What has just been said, applies equally to
small towns and their neighbouring lands, to large
manufacturing towns or districts, and the other
districts of the same nation, and to manufacturing
nations and agricultural nations. The commerce
between an agricultural and a manufacturing nation, is as mutually advantageous as the commerce in corn and cloth carried on between the
inhabitants of a town and the farmers in the
neighbourhood. If a free trade in corn and cloth
were allowed between England and France, the
art of agriculture would improve in France, and
the art of making cloth would improve in England; but the art of making cloth would remain
nearly stationary in France, and in England the
art of agriculture would make slow progress.
The mutual benefit which the two countries
would derive from such a free trade is indisputable, on the supposition, that such free trade
is not subject to interruptions; for every Englishman and Frenchman would then procure the ne-

cessaries of life with diminished labour ; and consequently, the wealth or power of both England and France would be increased. When there is a chance of interruption, the policy of allowing a free trade will depend on the decision of these two questions :—Whether the improvement in the agriculture of France, would compensate for the check given to the art of making cloth ; *and whether England's rapid advancement in the art of making cloths, would compensate for her slow advancement in agriculture?*

No useful commerce can exist between two very distant countries for any great length of time. The improvements made in the arts in one country, by means of the division of labour, and by means of large capitals, may be so great and so rapid, that this country may supply for a time many distant countries with manufactures. But when the arts in this country have nearly reached perfection, the expense of transporting the commodities exchanged, will be so great, that very high rewards will be conferred on those who succeed in transferring capital from this country to other countries ; these rewards will be so high, that it will be impossible for the rich country to prevent the export of workmen and machinery to other countries. All useful distant commerce is founded on inequality in the knowledge of the useful arts ;

and it is impossible to prevent this knowledge from diffusing itself. When the knowledge of the arts is equally diffused, nearly all commerce between distant towns will cease, and every country or small territory will be independent of all other countries. At no distant period, England will cease to manufacture for the rest of the world, and every nation will find it most profitable to manufacture for itself.

The chief engine or instrument of commerce, is shipping. The building of ships and navigating them, resolves itself into the labour of felling timber, transporting it to the dock-yards, constructing and equipping the ships, and providing the sailors with a little more than the necessaries of life. The division of labour cannot be carried to any greater extent in the art of ship-building, than it can in the art of agriculture ; so that a nation just rising in the arts, can produce and navigate a given quantity of shipping with nearly as little labour as a nation far advanced in the arts. If it be also taken into consideration, that timber is more easily procured in agricultural countries than in manufacturing countries, it may be affirmed as nearly true, that a given quantity of shipping may be produced and navigated by the same quantity of labour, in all nations. But a given quantity of gold will not represent the same quantity of shipping in all countries ; on the contrary, the more a nation is advanced in the arts, the cheaper is gold compared with labour, or the dearer is labour compared with gold. For instance, France may produce and navigate a ship for 200 ounces of gold a-year, which England could not produce and navigate for less than 300 ounces. Consequently, France must be continually driving England out of the ship-market wherever there is a free trade allowed. England will certainly benefit in some respects, by allowing this free trade in shipping ; for English merchants will have to pay only two ounces of gold to foreign ship-owners, where they would have to pay three ounces to English ship-owners ; and the labour which the English ship-builders would have expended on ships, being expended on manufactures, which will be sent to South America, or elsewhere, will exchange for three ounces of gold. But the policy of England's allowing a free trade in shipping depends on this : *whether the diminution of England's maritime superiority is not a greater evil than can be compensated by the temporary advantages arising from a free trade in shipping ?*

There are several kinds of useless commerce, some of which I shall now proceed to enumerate.

One of the commonest is that where manufactures are exchanged for gold. If the manufactures are necessaries, the party producing gold is engaged in a useful commerce; because he probably has found, that a given quantity of labour will produce gold, which will exchange for more clothing or machinery than that labour could have directly produced. But the party giving manufactures for gold, is almost always engaged in a useless commerce, for gold is seldom purchased in a foreign country for any other purpose than to exchange it for a luxury of some other foreign country. The country receiving gold, does no more than barter luxuries for luxuries, through the medium of gold. The labour expended on such commerce, is not however unmixed with some degree of utility; for the labour expended on the ships and home manufactures sent abroad, tends to improve the useful arts of ship-building and manufacturing, and is, on that account, more useful than the labour of domestic servants. England is rather benefitted by the residence of her rich men in other countries; for when these men return home, a great portion of the labour now engaged in producing manufactures to be exchanged for gold, will be expended on domestic services. All Englishmen residing in France, and all Irishmen residing in England, are supported by the labour of the people from whom they receive their rents.

The exchange of manufactures for wines is a very useless and even a pernicious commerce in most cases. England exchanges her manufactures for gold, and this gold for wine. The more there is of wine consumed in England, the less will there be consumed of malt liquors. The effect of a free trade in wine is to give a stimulus to the arts of manufacturing, and to check the progress of the art of agriculture. Inasmuch, therefore, as improvements in the art of agriculture are of far greater national utility than improvements in the manufacturing arts, it is the duty of the English national government to discourage the free trade in wine.

The trade in sugar, tea, coffee, &c., is also useless, but it tends indirectly, in a very slight degree, to increase the power or wealth of a nation. The slight degree of utility attending this commerce, arises from the effect it produces in the improvement of the useful arts. On account of this commerce, a greater quantity of labour is engaged in the useful arts of ship-building and manufacturing, than would be required for the useful commerce in necessaries. If this commerce were put an end to, a large portion of this additional labour would be expended in domestic services, and in manufacturing arts of the lowest degree of utility. The improvement of any art depends, in a great measure, on the quantity of labour engaged in that art. Most of the foreign, and part of the domestic commerce of England, is no farther useful, than as it increases the labour expended on the useful arts, and diminishes the labour expended on domestic services and the useless arts.

It requires no deep penetration to discover that a free trade in machinery is very injurious to the exporting country. If a manufacturing nation can, by expending a given quantity of labour directly on the soil, obtain more corn than other nations are ready to give it, for the manufactures produced by the same quantity of labour, in such a case, (which never did occur,) machinery might be freely exported with advantage. But, of two nations trading with each other in corn and cloth, the chief advantage of such commerce lies, in most cases, on the side of the manufacturing nation. In all cases, the manufacturing nation must be a gainer by such commerce ; and, in all cases, the agricultural nation loses the labour expended on the transport of their corn to the manufacturing nation. It is to save this labour of transport that the agricultural nation will offer high rewards for the transfer of machinery, and the

necessary labourers, or capital, from the manufacturing nations. These rewards will at last be
so high, that it will be impossible for the manufacturing nation to prevent the export of their
capital. *But that nation acts most foolishly which
joins her own efforts to those of other nations, to
deprive herself of the advantages she is enjoying,
by allowing a free trade in machinery and ar-
tisans.*

CHAPTER III.

On the Size of Towns.

MEN collect themselves into villages or towns,
on account of the saving of labour effected by
the division of labour. The larger a town becomes, the farther removed are the inhabitants
from the lands which supply them with corn;
and the labour of transporting the corn from the
country to the town, is by so much increased.
The larger a town is, the more may the labour
expended on manufactures be divided; and consequently the more labour may be saved. The
towns of a nation will have attained their proper
size when an increase of the population causes no
greater saving, by the division of labour, than it

causes loss, by the additional labour required to transport corn and manure to and from the town and country. In countries far advanced in the useful arts, the population of such towns will probably be some number between 500 and 5000. The towns of England seldom produce their own clothing; most of the towns are dependent on a few of the towns for their supply of clothing and machinery. It is, however, extremely probable, that when the useful manufacturing arts have nearly reached perfection, it will be found most advantageous for every town to produce its own clothing and plain machinery. Of the populations of English towns, a very small portion is engaged in the production of necessaries or wealth; and of the labour so employed, one-half, if properly applied, would be sufficient to produce as much as is now produced by the whole. Take, for example, the bakers of any town: there is no room for doubting, that if half the baking capitals existing in any town, were united together under one head, the bread produced would be at least equal to the bread produced by all the capitals acting separately. These capitals have a natural tendency to unite together, but they are prevented by the pernicious laws which uphold the vicious system of private competition.

It will be useful to obtain an approximation
to the quantities of labour expended on the transport of food and manure, to and from towns of
different sizes. We will first take a town with
a population of 500, the agriculturists being supposed to reside in the town. We will suppose
that each individual requires an acre of land for
his support; that each individual consumes two
pounds of corn a-day; that each town is the
centre of a circular country from which its food
is raised; that the weight of the manure taken
from the town is equal to that of the corn brought
from the country; and that a load for three horses
is about fifteen hundred weight. This town, then,
of 500 inhabitants, will be supplied by a circle,
whose area is 500 acres, whose radius or semi-
diameter, consequently, is 880 yards, and whose
produce amounts to about 200 loads of corn, the
manure required being also 200 loads.   Now
part of these 400 loads must be carried the distance of the whole radius, or 880 yards, part
only from just without the town.   It will appear,
on calculation, that the mean distance at which
the whole of the corn and manure may be sup-
posed to be carried is $\frac{2}{3} \times 880$ yards, or one-third
of a mile.   That is, this whole labour of transport
resolves itself into 400 loads carried one-third of
a mile, or into one load carried 140 miles.

If the population were increased to one thousand, the annual amount in corn and manure would be 800 loads; but the average distance which each load must be carried, would be increased in the proportion of the radius of the circle, whose area is one thousand acres, to the radius of the circle whose area is 500 acres; that is, in the proportion of the square root of two to unity, or of 1.414 to unity. Consequently, if the whole amount of labour necessary to transport food and manure for towns of 500 and 1000 inhabitants, were equally divided amongst the inhabitants; then the labour required of the man belonging to the town of 500, would be to that required of the man of the town of 1000 inhabitants, as 1 : 1.414. If the town of 500 were increased to 5000, the portions of labour required for the same purpose of an inhabitant of each town, would be as $1 : \sqrt{10}$, that is as 1 : 3.163. The amount of labour required to transport food and manure to and from the town of 5000 inhabitants, will be that of carrying one load $140 \times 10 \times 3.163$ miles, or 3428 miles. What has just been said of the labour of conveying food to towns of different sizes, is applicable to armies of different sizes. For instance, suppose an army of 10,000 men to draw its supplies from the surrounding country, by means of the labour of one hundred horses and men; then to supply an army of 100,000 men, $100 \times 10 \times \sqrt{10}$, or 3163 horses and men will be required.

If the food of each individual of the towns be spread over a surface of two acres, the above-mentioned labour of transport will be doubled. The same is true of armies: the labour of subsisting a given army is directly proportional to the rarity with which this food is spread over a country.

The effect of placing a town by the sea-shore, or on the banks of a wide river, is the making it draw its supplies of food from a country in the form of a semicircle, instead of a circle, and thus increasing the labour of transporting food and manure in the proportion of $\sqrt{2}$ to unity. But in English towns, where the consumption of coal is great, this disadvantage is more than compensated by the saving in the carriage of coals. Suppose, for instance, each family to consume annually one hundred bushels of coals, that is, about a load of 15 cwt. each individual, or 500 loads for a town of 500 inhabitants. The propriety of having the country near the town in the form of a circle or semicircle, will depend on which is most laborious; to transport 400 loads 587 yards, and 500 loads 880 yards, or to transport 400 loads 587 × $\sqrt{2}$ or 830 yards: the advantage is evidently on the side of the semicircular form of the country. If, however, fuel were economized as much as it might be, the most advantageous form of the country round a town would be that of a circle.

CHAPTER IV.

On the Measure of Value.

I HAVE affixed the rather vague term "measure of value" to the head of the present chapter, because, in its present acceptation, it will indicate the matter I now propose to consider. By the measure of value, I would be understood to mean some scale or standard, real or fictitious, to which all commodities may be referred. The higher any article ranks on this scale, the more useful, precious, or desirable, is it considered to be.

Wherever the money system prevails, it is very evident, that among individuals of the same country, money is the measure of value: an article which will exchange for twice as much money as another, being generally supposed to be twice as desirable, and a man who can command twice as much money as another being generally twice as powerful. But for the national value of commodities, money is no standard at all. A certain quantity of lace will represent the same sum of money, as a certain quantity of corn ; and perhaps the lace has cost as much labour as the corn : but the lace is of no national utility because it cannot, like the corn, maintain labourers in the arts of war, agriculture, or other useful arts. Nor is money by any means a correct standard of the national value of necessaries. The money price of a certain quantity of corn, and a certain number of muskets, may be the same, although the muskets may have cost twice as much labour as the corn. If the corn be produced by half the quantity of labour which produced the muskets, (which is very probable,) then the national value of the corn is only half that of the muskets.

All commodities, all necessaries and luxuries, are the effects of labour,—labour is the price paid for all commodities. Since, therefore, labour and commodities stand in the relation of cause and effect, labour is the natural measure of value ; this supposing nothing more than, that effects are proportional to their causes. If the effects produced by a given quantity of labour were the same in all countries, then the labour of one man for a given time would be a correct universal measure of value. But in different nations, a given quantity of labour produces different effects : the effect produced depends chiefly on the arts ; the more advanced the nation is in the arts, the greater is the effect produced by a given quantity of labour. For this reason, the labour of a man in England for a given time, will produce a considerably greater quantity of corn and clothing than the labour of a Frenchman for the same time, the soil being of the same quality in both cases. The excess of the effect of an Englishman's labour over that of a. Spaniard is still greater. In every part of the same nation, the effect produced by a given quantity of labour is the same very nearly. Hence the true national standard of value for all commodities, is the labour of one man of that nation for a given time. If, however, commodities are compared together with respect to their national value, or to their effects in producing national power, luxuries are to be excluded from the comparison, and necessaries alone are to be compared by this standard.

There is, I believe, a tolerably correct universal measure of value for all commodities; which is,— a given quantity of corn. The national measure of value, is the labour of a man of that nation for a given time: the universal measure of value must therefore be some commodity which is produced by the same quantity of labour in all countries, whether they have made much or little progress in the arts. If the labour bestowed on a certain space of land be doubled, the produce of that land will be less than doubled, supposing no improved modes of applying labour to have been discovered; but if the art of agriculture has been improved, it is not improbable that twice the labour will produce twice the quantity of corn, and three times the labour three times the quantity of corn. The labour bestowed on a given space of land, is seldom increased before the art of agriculture has been improved. It may be said, that the labour bestowed on a given space of land, continually increasing in a certain ratio, the produce of that land continually increases in a lower ratio. It may be assumed, as near the truth, that the progress of the art of agriculture is such as, by improved applications of labour, will render the lower increasing ratio equal to the former increasing ratio. In this case, a given quantity of labour will produce a given quantity of corn in all countries, *and a given quantity of corn will be a universal measure of value.*

Commodities are measured by labour, but labour itself is measured by necessaries; for a certain quantity of necessaries will generally represent or command as much labour as it can maintain, whether it be the labour of men or of horses. It has been shown, that in countries advanced as far as England in the arts, the constant labour of

one man is sufficient to provide the necessaries of
life for three families, the food being corn.
Hence, a man's labour in England costs the third
part of the produce of his labour, if it be expended on necessaries; or the third part of the
same quantity of labour, bestowed on necessaries,
which he bestows on luxuries.   If English labourers lived on potatoes, their labour would not
cost so much as the tenth-part of their labour;
and their masters would have nine-tenths instead
of two-thirds of their labour available.   The
labour of a horse in England, by the instrumentality of one acre of land, costs about one-tenth
of its labour.

We have seen, that labour is the national
measure of value.   Money is, in some degree, a
measure of value, for it is generally true that the
article which costs most money also costs most
labour.   I shall now proceed to exhibit the causes
of money not being an accurate measure of value.
Money is prevented from becoming a correct national standard of value by the action of the division of labour on the system of profits of capital.
If there existed no profits on capital, money would
be a correct national measure of value.   Again, if
every commodity were produced and prepared for
consumption by a single distinct capital, then
money would be a correct measure of all commo-

dities, whatever might be the general rate of profit on capital. But no commodity is prepared for consumption by any one capital: corn, for example, is prepared for consumption by the separate capitals of the farmer, the corn-factor, and the baker, to these may be added the capitals of the wheelwright, of the horse-dealer, of the road-maker, of the house-builder, &c., all of which are engaged in the preparation of corn for the use of the consumer. Cloth is probably prepared for the consumer by yet a greater number of capitals. If there were no profit on capital, the money price of all articles would be proportional to the labour expended on their production. But under the system of profits, the money price of a commodity is made up of two parts, one of which is paid to the labour which produced it, the other part is paid to the commanders of that labour, and is called profit. The part which pays profits is very variable; of some commodities, half the price is paid as profits; of other commodities, two-thirds is paid as profit. The general law is, that the greater the number of capitals through which any article passes before it reaches the consumer, the greater proportion of the whole price is paid as profits. A little reflection will make this manifest. I will, however, give an illustration of the principle. Suppose, for example, that a certain commodity passes through the hands of seven traders;—that the first alone expends any considerable quantity of labour on its production, and that 10 per cent. is the ordinary rate of profit. Suppose the first to spend 100*l.* in labour, then he will charge 110*l.* for the article to the second trader; the second will charge 121*l.* to the third, and so on to the seventh, who will charge the consumer 200*l.* for the commodity. Thus the whole price will be made up of half paid as wages, and half paid as profits. It is manifest, that if the number of traders were increased, the proportion of profits would be increased.

There is a prejudice existing in the minds of most men, the removal of which would be productive of important advantages to the world in general. The prejudice I allude to, is the regarding gold as the universal measure of power: those nations are supposed to be most wealthy, which have most gold; it is, however, not improbable, that the poorest nations are those which have most gold. Experience has shown, that all nations producing gold have been poor and powerless; nations advanced in the arts can draw this gold to them at their pleasure; these rich nations barter the gold obtained from the poor nations for the commodities of other nations: the interchange of their own commodities being performed through the instrumentality of paper-money.   A rich nation, by retaining much gold as money, will by that means diminish its riches.   Gold, like all other commodities, is the effect of labour, and may be measured by the universal standard of value— a given quantity of corn.   If in a certain country the gold price of corn be greater than in other countries, it is improper to say, that corn is dear in that country ; we should rather say, that gold is cheap in that country ; for a given quantity of corn costs the same quantity of labour in all nations.   If a given quantity of corn, which costs an ounce of gold in Poland, cost two ounces in England, then gold is twice as cheap in England as in Poland.

It remains to account for the different degrees of cheapness of gold in different countries.   Experience shows us the cause of gold being more or less cheap.   If we look round the world we shall find this general law prevailing,—the farther the arts have advanced in any country, the cheaper is gold in that country.   For example, England has advanced farther in the arts, or is more powerful than France ; a given quantity of corn, therefore, in England represents more gold than it does in France ; again, France is farther advanced than any of the rest of European nations, gold is therefore cheapest there.   I shall now proceed to show, that these facts are the consequences of the principles laid down. It may be assumed, with sufficient accuracy, that of two quantities of corn and cloth of equal money value in France, the true value or the labour value of the corn is to the true value of the cloth, in the same proportion as the true values of similar quantities of corn and cloth are in England. Suppose, now, that in England, a given quantity of corn is of equal exchangeable value with three yards of cloth, whilst in France the same corn will only exchange for two yards of cloth of the same quality; we should say, then, that cloth is cheaper in England than in France, in the proportion of three to two. But a given quantity of this cloth will command, or will be exchanged for, a given quantity of gold in the foreign nations to which England and France may trade. Three pieces of gold will be returned for the three yards of English cloth, and two pieces of gold for the two yards of French cloth. It follows then, that gold is cheaper in England than in France in the proportion of three to two, or that a given quantity of corn will exchange for as much and half as much more gold in England as it will in France, because cloth is cheaper in that proportion. An ounce of gold represents, or will command, the same quantity of cloth in England as in France; so that cloth may be regarded as always convertible into gold. We may then say, generally, that the cheaper cloth is in any country, the cheaper is gold, or the higher is the price of food in that country.

It is of importance to nations and individuals, who have to make fixed annual gold payments, to know the relation of gold to that universal standard,—a given quantity of corn. If (which is probable) the same labour is required to produce one quarter of wheat, as is required to produce half an ounce of gold; then, with the progress of the arts, and with the diminution of profits throughout the world, the price of a quarter of wheat in all countries will tend to become equal to that of half an ounce of gold. In England, for example, in 1840, an ounce of gold will probably not command more than half as much corn as it did in 1810; and, consequently, a given sum of money, convertible into gold, will be twice as difficult to raise, since it will cost twice as much labour.

CHAPTER V.

Pauperism.

IT has been shown, in the chapter on population, that a people, under favourable circumstances, will double itself in twenty years. If any population increase so rapidly, they will soon arrive at that natural limit, beyond which the power of sustenance residing in the land does not permit them to pass. If the number of the population exceed this limit prescribed by nature, the excess is carried off by the increased mortality caused by semi-starvation. A people in such a state, may be said to be suffering under natural pauperism; their pauperism would be similar to that suffered by all the lower animals, which are constantly pressing against the bounds of subsistence. But this natural pauperism exists in no European nation; there is hardly a country in Europe, whose lands are not capable of sustaining ten times as many people as they do sustain.

European pauperism originates in the institution of private property, and the separation of men into two classes, masters and labourers. The minds of the class of labourers are so uncultivated, that their principles of action are

very similar to those of horses or other beasts
of burden; the labourer, like the horse, works
hard for the bare necessaries of life, and his
master enjoys the greater part of the produce of
his labour : the labourer, like the horse, is always
ready to propagate, although he knows he must
thereby bring semi-starvation on himself and
family. The class of labourers consists of two
parts, one of which is engaged in the production of necessaries for themselves and the rest
of the population, the other part is engaged in
the production of luxuries for the enjoyment of
the class of masters. The former part are the
producers of national wealth or necessaries; the
latter part and class of masters are the consumers of the national wealth only, and are
consequently of little or no national utility.
The useful part of the class of labourers, in a
country advanced as far as England in the arts,
forms about the third part of the entire population. The chief necessary of life is food, and
the labour required to produce the other necessaries of life is comparatively so inconsiderable,
that a very insignificant error will be committed,
by supposing that food or corn is the only necessary of life. It will then follow, that English
pauperism commences when, by the cultivation
of inferior lands, the constant labour of one man
is insufficient to provide corn for himself and two

men more, (considering the aggregate effect of
the labour expended on all lands.) French pauperism probably commences when the constant
labour of one Frenchman becomes insufficient to
provide food for himself and one man more.

All old nations have arrived at this kind of
pauperism, where the farther increase of the population is limited,—not by the power of each
man to sustain himself, but by the power of each
man to sustain one or two men besides himself.
In England, the class of masters extract from the
useful labourers two-thirds of the necessaries produced by them, by means of revenues on lands and
houses, and by profits on fixed and current labour.
The masters retain for their own consumption, the
half of the necessaries thus obtained ; the other
half, they expend on the maintenance of labour to
prepare luxuries for them. There are two ways
only in which such populations can increase : one
is, when by means of improvement in the useful
arts, the useful part of the population are enabled
to produce an increased quantity of necessaries ;
the other way is, when, by the diminution of the
general rate of revenue and profit, the proportion
of useless labourers becomes diminished, and the
proportion of useful labourers increased. These
two causes are operating, though slowly, in all
European countries. *The rate of increase of a
population is proportional to the rapidity with*

which the rate of profit diminishes, and to the rapidity of its progress in the useful arts.

It has been said, that labourers, like the lower animals, are continually pressing against the bounds of subsistence. The truth of this assertion may be doubted by some, because labourers frequently enjoy luxuries: they will however perceive, on observing more closely, that labourers can seldom purchase luxuries, except by depriving themselves of the necessaries of life. In an old country, the wages of labour may represent more than the necessaries of life for a short period; but the abundance of necessaries has been invariably followed by a scarcity of necessaries for the labourer. Taking the wages of labour in all European countries, in all ages, it will be found that they have, for a much longer period, represented an insufficiency, than they have a sufficiency, of the necessaries of life, for a man and his family. Labourers, nevertheless, have it in their power to raise the wages of labour to such an amount, as to represent an abundance of the necessaries of life. Labourers can live without the help of masters; but labourers are necessary for the existence of masters. If labourers were to cease to propagate so rapidly and heedlessly, the number of labourers would be diminished, and the masters would enter into competition for the labourers, who would sell themselves to the highest bidders.

The class of labourers may secure to themselves high real wages, by keeping the supply of labourers a little below the demand, or by refraining from marrying when wages are low. The cause of pauperism is, the supply of labourers exceeding the demand.

When the supply of labourers exceeds the demand, (that is, in England, when a man is not able to produce three times as much necessaries as he can consume,) the whole amount of necessaries divided among the labourers will remain unchanged, and consequently the average quantity received by each labourer will be diminished. By the diminution of the necessaries, or by semi-starvation of the labourer, the mortality among the labourers will be increased, and the supply of labourers will be reduced to a level with the demand, unless the excess be maintained by improvident propagation. It unfortunately happens, that in all countries, labourers are so little above the level of the brutes, that the supply of labourers always exceeds the demand for them. There is this difference between the methods pursued by England and other countries, for preventing the excess of labourers above the demand. In England, this excess is kept in check, by diminishing the necessaries of a part only of the labourers, which part receives parish pay; in other countries, this excess is checked, by the diminution of the general rate of wages, and consequently by diminishing the necessaries of all labourers.

All men consume the same quantity of necessaries: a rich man consumes no more necessaries than a poor man; he has only, added to his necessaries, a certain quantity of luxuries. The difference between a master and labourer consists in this: the master has the command of the necessaries he requires for his own consumption, and of the necessaries of one or two more men, which he cannot consume, for which he is compelled to do nothing: the labourer cannot get possession of the necessaries, which the master cannot consume, except by labouring according to his master's pleasure, either in the production of necessaries or luxuries. The price paid for all luxuries is necessaries. A master who purchases a luxury does nothing more than transfer the command he has over necessaries to the labourers who produced that luxury. A man who spends a thousand pounds a-year in luxuries, does no more than exchange the necessaries which he cannot consume, for luxuries which he can consume. If 30*l.* a-year be considered as representing the necessaries of life required by a man and his family; then a man with a revenue of 30*l.* a-year will command the necessaries he requires and nothing more: a man having 60*l.* a-year will command the necessaries and consequently the labour of another man, which labour will appear in the

form of luxuries. Suppose, now, that a man having 60*l.* a-year, were to divide it into two parcels
of 30*l.* each, and keep one parcel for himself, and
give the other to his eldest son, who has a family;
the consequence will be, that the labourer who
produced luxuries for the man of 60*l.* a-year, will
be driven out of existence by the man to whom
the 30*l.* is given. The more a certain amount of
revenue is divided, the greater proportion of that
revenue is consumed by people who do nothing.
Every division of a revenue drives a labourer on
luxuries out of existence.

What has been said, is sufficient to show, that
in case the class of masters should choose to diminish their luxuries, by portioning out their children, the class of labourers would be forced into
pauperism, even if they produced no more children than sufficient to maintain their numbers stationary. This probably is the case throughout all
countries in some degree; the lowest class of labourers are made paupers, partly by their own
thoughtless increase, and partly by the increase of
the higher class of labourers and masters. Pauperism is occasioned by the population being
greater than the necessaries produced can sustain.
The best way to keep population on a level with
necessaries, or the best cure for pauperism, is a tax
on propagation, or a tax on the marriages both of

masters and labourers.   In England, where there
is very little propagation without marriage, a tax
on marriages would be sufficient : the tax should
increase with the proportion of paupers : — a
month's income of every marrying man might be
a good tax to begin with.   Such a tax would be
an efficient antagonist to the pernicious laws made
every where for the stimulating of propagation,
which laws cannot suddenly be repealed with
safety.

CHAPTER VI.

Revenue and Wages.

THE income of every individual consists either
of Revenue or Wages, or of both.   Revenue is
what costs the receiver no labour, it is generally
derived from property in lands, houses, money,
machinery, &c.   Wages may be defined to be the
commodities which a man of ordinary talents, and
possessing no property or credit, receives in exchange for his labour.   Wages, according to this
definition, are nothing more than the necessaries
required for the subsistence of the labourer, or a
sum of money representing these necessaries.
Day labourers, or the lowest class of labourers,

live entirely on wages: a small number of men
live on revenue solely : the majority of the English population lives partly on revenue and
partly on wages. The people who form this
middling class are agents, servants of the higher
order, mechanics, tradesmen, and professional men.
The salary of an agent or of a superior servant, is
not paid for his labour only ; for there are always
many men, able and willing to perform the same
duties, for the necessaries of life, or the ordinary
wages of labour. The excess of an agent's or a
servant's salary above the ordinary wages of labour, is paid to him as revenue for the insuring of
his fidelity. If men in responsible situations received no more than labourer's wages, they would
be easily tempted to commit a breach of trust or
confidence, for the chance of bettering their condi_
tion. Professional men, like agents, receive high
salaries, because great trust is reposed in them.
The rest of the middling class, consists of those
who manage their own small or large property.
A tradesman or manufacturer may realize a profit
of 1000*l.* a-year, but no more than 30*l.* of this
sum ought to be regarded as wages of labour, because one of the labourers of the tradesman or
manufacturer would conduct the business equally
well for that sum ; the remainder of the profit
970*l.* must be considered as revenue, since it is

the effect of property and not of labour. A mechanic will derive a considerable revenue from his
small property in tools. Of properties employed in
the different orders of trade, the smaller properties yield a higher rate of revenue than the larger:
thus, a mechanic reaps a higher rate of revenue
from his small property than the inn-keeper, the
inn-keeper a higher rate than the retail dealer
in clothes, the retail dealer a higher rate than the
wholesale dealer in clothes. All profits are almost
wholly composed of revenue. The revenue of a
property employed in trade is generally four times
greater than that of an equal property out of
trade. That is to say, the ordinary rate of profit
is to the ordinary rate of interest of money, as
four to *one*.

It has been shown, that the necessaries for the
whole English population are produced by the
labour of the third part of that population:
there remains, then, two-thirds of the necessaries
of life to be received as revenue. All English
revenue represents nothing more than the necessaries, or the luxuries which the labour maintained by these necessaries has produced. The
English population may be supposed, as in the
last chapter, to be divided into three equal parts,
viz. useful labourers, useless labourers, and masters. The first two parts receive nothing but

wages, or the necessaries of life, the third part, or
the masters, receive their share of the necessaries of
life, and the luxuries produced by the useless labourers. The income of every labourer will represent
the third part of the produce of his labour, the income of every master will represent four-thirds of
the effects of a man's labour. My business will now
be to show in what manner the process of extract-
ing necessaries from the producers of those necessaries is carried on. It may be supposed, without occasioning but a very trifling error, that
corn is the only necessary which men consume ;
the consumption of houses, machines, clothes, &c.,
being inconsiderable when compared with the
necessary consumption of corn. The useful labourers will then produce three times as much corn
as they consume ; two-thirds of the corn they produce is taken from them in the form of revenue.

There are two kinds of revenue taken from
the producers of the corn. One kind of revenue
is that which may be called arbitrary revenue,
the other kind of revenue is that usually termed
profits of capital, but which is nothing more than
a revenue which capitalists derive from managing the fixed or current labour which they
command. Of the first kind are tithes, rent of
land, and taxes paid to government pensioners.
The revenue of the pensioners is very inconsi-

derable, compared with other revenues : we will, however, suppose this revenue to be the *thirtieth* part of the whole produce. The next kind of arbitrary revenue is tithes, which we may take to amount to the tenth part of the revenue. The rent of land partakes, in some measure, of the nature of the revenue from capital; for all improved lands contain a great deal of fixed labour. Since, however, this fixed labour has not been expended by the proprietors of land, but by farmers ; and since a fertile soil, yielding a high rent, does not necessarily contain any fixed labour, I have here chosen to class rent of land among arbitrary revenues. In England, the rent of land has been stated to amount to the *fifth* part of the whole produce ; consequently we shall have, for the amount of the three kinds of arbitrary revenue, *one-third of all the corn produced.*

The revenue derived from capital comes next to be considered. The revenue exacted by the farmer for the use of the current and the fixed labour, which he commands and manages, cannot be estimated at less than the *ninth* part of the whole produce. The revenue which the farmer pays to horse-dealers, to manufacturers of farming implements, to insurance offices, &c., may be taken to amount to the *ninth* part of the produce ; and the revenues paid for the use of

houses, with other revenues paid by the agricultural labourer, may be considered as amounting
to another *ninth* part of the produce; we shall
then have three-ninths, or one-third of all corn,
taken as revenue of capital, which, with the third
part taken as arbitrary revenue, makes up *two-
thirds of all corn produced expended as revenue.*

Rent is the consideration which farmers pay for
the use of land, with the view of realizing the
ordinary rate of profit on capital, or twenty-five
per cent. per annum. Whatever they expect to
get more than this, they will engage to pay as
rent or revenue to their landlords. Hence the
variations of rents: the farmer's profits are constant, being the same as equal capitals engaged
in any other trade; but the rents vary with the
fertility of the soil, and with the distance of the
lands from market or from manure. The most
sterile land in cultivation yields no rent, the most
fertile land the greatest rent. Tithes are a tax
on rent: on good and improved land they produce no effect, different from the effect of rents,
on the farmer and labourer; to the landholder
they diminish his rents by their whole amount.
Tithes prevent the bringing of poor land into
cultivation, and likewise obstruct the improvement of land already in cultivation. If there
were no tithes, all land would be cultivated,

which would yield the farmer the ordinary profits
of capital. In a country where tithes are paid,
no land can be cultivated which will not yield the
rent of tithes, in addition to the farmer's ordinary
profit. The effects of such a system, in checking the
increase of agricultural produce, and consequently in
checking the increase of the population, are manifest. These evils might be remedied by a legislative
enactment, ordering the tithes to bear a certain fixed
proportion to the rent, as *one-fourth* or *one-fifth*.

It has been seen, that in England, two-thirds
of the necessaries produced by the useful labourers
are consumed as revenue; and I have supposed
the consumers of revenue to be divided into two
equal parts, masters and useless labourers. It remains to explain the manner in which money
effects the distribution of necessaries to every
individual of the population, and of luxuries to
the third part of the population. It may be assumed of all commodities, both necessaries and
luxuries, as generally true, that the price paid
by the consumer is made up of one-third paid as
wages, and two-thirds paid as revenue. If, for
example, the price to the consumer for a certain
quantity of corn be three shillings, it may be taken
for granted, that one shilling only has been expended on the labourers who produced the corn,
the remaining two shillings having been taken as

revenue by people who have and have not been engaged in the management of the labour which produced the corn. The same is true of most luxuries, only one-third of the consumer's price is paid to labourers ; the remainder is swallowed up as revenue by those who may be called useless capitalists, through whose hands articles pass before they reach the consumer. It may be assumed, that 25*l.* a-year represents the necessaries consumed by every family, rich and poor, that is, at the rate of 5*l.* a-year each individual. A useful labourer will then produce luxuries represented by 75*l.* a-year. But since the excess of labourers' productions over 25*l.* a-year goes to masters, every master corresponding to two labourers will receive necessaries and luxuries represented by 100*l.* a-year. The income of every three of the population will then amount to 150*l.* a-year, that is, if equally divided, 50*l.* each family, or 10*l.* a-year each individual. It will probably be found, that the average annual consumption of necessaries and luxuries in England, is about 10*l.* each person.

The class of useful and useless capitalists, are to be considered as partly labourers and partly masters. The rate of revenue from capitals very little affects capitalists among each other : if one capitalist receive a revenue of ten per cent. on his capital, he must also pay a revenue of ten per cent. to other capitalists. But the case is far different with men living on fixed incomes without labour. If there were no revenue from capital, a man with a fixed income of 75*l.* a-year, would command the luxuries produced by three men: but owing to the revenue on capital, such a man will not command the produce of more than one man's labour; the capitalists will keep for themselves the produce of the other two men's labour. Men of large property, may greatly increase their power or wealth, by repealing the laws which prevent the diminution of the rate of revenue derived from trading capitals.

Revenue is a tax on labour. There can be no additional tax imposed on labourers. Labourers, like horses, give all their labour for the necessaries of life. The taxing of wages would be nothing more than taking away the necessaries of life from the labourer. This tax exists only when the supply of labourers exceeds the demand; and the tax cures the evil, by diminishing the population. The amount of money wages, is of the most trivial importance: it matters not whether a labourer receives his daily bread through the medium of a penny or a shilling. The real wages of labour are generally constant; when prices rise, money wages rise; when prices fall, money wages fall.

CHAPTER VII.

Profits of Capital, and Interest of Money.

I HAVE defined capital, as consisting in the current and fixed labour engaged in the pro-duction of necessaries. The current and fixed labour employed by a man to produce luxuries *not* for his own consumption, is commonly called capital: I would distinguish it from the other, by calling it useless capital. The current labour, of which capital is composed, may be represented by the necessaries which sustain this labour; the fixed labour, or the machinery and stock, forming part of capital, may be represented by the neces-saries which have sustained this past and now fixed labour: all capitals might then be measured by a given quantity of necessaries. Stock is the effect of machinery and current labour; and for that reason the two constituent parts of capital may be considered to be, machinery and current labour. Machinery also is the effect of current labour; but capital cannot be considered as con-sisting of current labour alone, because the current labour producing machinery, remains for a very long time: as for stock, it is consumed soon after it is produced. It may be assumed, as tolerably

near the truth, that the effect of labour, fixed in
land or other machinery, engaged in the useful
arts, is such, that the labour of one man in this
way for a year, is sufficient to produce as much as
the perpetual labour of one man, without any
farther expense; and that there is an idle man,
or a liver on revenue, to every such quantity of
fixed labour. Thus, if the useful fixed labour in
England be the effect of the labour of two-thirds
of the population for a year, or be represented by
the necessaries of two-thirds of the population for
a year, then this fixed labour or machinery will
save the labour of two-thirds of the population
for ever, and this part of the population will be
livers on revenue. Every equal population consumes very nearly the same quantity of necessaries; consequently, on the supposition I have
just made, the useful capitals of all equal populations are equal. In a nation which has made
little progress in the arts, the useful capital consists almost wholly of current labour: in a nation
far advanced in the arts, the useful capital is
chiefly in machinery: the capital of a rich nation
costs little necessaries to maintain it, because the
greater part of it is fixed labour; the capital of a
poor nation costs much necessaries, because it
consists chiefly of current labour. The commodities which constitute riches, are generally as

abundant in poor nations as in rich nations;—necessaries are riches: but what distinguishes a
powerful nation from a weak nation, is the facility
with which necessaries are procured;—*the nation
which produces a given quantity of necessaries with
least labour, is the most powerful.* A nation like
England, which can procure the necessaries, plain
food, clothing, and lodging of the whole population, by means of the labour of the third part of
the population, may expend the labour of the remaining two-thirds in the arts of war. But in
all nations, a very inconsiderable portion of the
labour saved in the production of other necessaries, is expended on the necessaries of war.
The labour saved is, for the most part, expended
in the production of luxuries: a great part of it
forms what I have designated useless capital.

Capital engaged in any one trade, cannot, without great difficulty, be transferred to any other
trade. Almost the only transferable part of capital is current labour: the machinery of one kind
of capital can rarely be converted into machinery
of another kind. That part of capital which is
most easily transferable is the current labour of
horses, or the necessaries which sustain the horses.
The current labour of men cannot easily be transferred from one capital to another, because a
man cannot learn a new art in less than two or

three years. For example, an agricultural capital
cannot be all converted into a war capital : the labour fixed in improved lands, and in other agricultural machines, cannot be converted into war
machines, such as ships, fortifications, and the machinery in dock-yards and arsenals. An agricultural labourer cannot be made a good soldier, or
sailor, or ship-builder, or iron-founder, in less than
two or three years. The necessaries expended on
a man learning an art may be considered as lost;
if a man learns two arts instead of one, he will occasion twice as great a national loss as was necessary.   The only part of agricultural capital which
can be readily converted into a war capital, is the
current labour of horses.

Profits are, as we have seen, resolvable into
revenue and wages ; and since wages form but a
very small portion of profits, it may be said, with
tolerable correctness, *that profit is the revenue of
managed capital.* All revenue is derived from
capital ; if any revenue be not obtained immediately from capital, it must be obtained by taxing
the revenue directly obtained from capital. If
there were no arbitrary revenue, as tithes, and
taxes for the support of government pensioners,
there would be no revenue but that directly from
capital. The direct revenue from capital is diminished by the whole amount of the arbitrary reve-

nue. The total revenue of any country is the difference between the whole of the necessaries produced, and that part of these necessaries consumed by the labourers who produced these necessaries. Rents, profits, tithes, and taxes, are the instruments by which the revenue is distributed. If rents are high, profits, tithes, and taxes must be low; if profits increase, rents, tithes, and taxes must diminish. Profits and rents agree together in this—they are both revenues derived from capital; but they differ from each other in this—rent is the revenue obtained by lending fixed labour to another, profit is the revenue derived from the management and command of fixed and current labour. If the management of capital cost no more than ordinary labour, then every man's direct revenue would be proportional to his capital, or to the necessaries which have been expended on the production of his capital. That is to say, if there were no profits, it would not happen, as it does now, that a certain property engaged in trade yields four times as much revenue as an equal property in lands, houses, &c. The difference between the rate of revenue from managed and unmanaged capital is gained as profit, and lost as rent. It is the interest of all men who live on the revenues from land and houses, that is, *it is the interest of the most wealthy and powerful men of a country, to diminish the rate of profits, or revenue from managed capital.* To produce this effect, no new laws are required ; nothing more is necessary than to abolish some old laws which fetter capital, and to guard all kinds of property by simple and impartial laws.

There is a natural tendency in all capitals to unite together and form one great capital, under one head or government.   This tendency is, in a great measure, the effect of the principle termed the " division of labour."   The cause of this tendency is the fact, that a certain quantity of fixed and current labour always produces a greater effect when united, than when it is divided into two or more parts.   Of two capitals engaged in the same trade, in the same place, it frequently happens, that the capital which is twice as great as the other, realizes twice the rate of profit ; it always happens, that the larger capital obtains a higher rate of profit than the smaller one. If two bakers in any town, having each a capital of 1000*l.*, were to unite their capitals, it is probable the united capital of 2000*l.* will yield a profit of thirty per cent. per annum, if the divided capitals before yielded twenty per cent. profit.   Two small proprietor-farmers are naturally inclined to unite their capitals, because they perceive that their capitals, when united, will produce a considerably greater effect than they do acting separately. By the increase of the size, or amount of single capitals, the national wealth or power is increased; because by this increase a greater quantity of commodities may be produced by a given quantity of labour. It does not follow, as a necessary consequence of the increased size of capitals, that the rate of profit will be diminished—such, however, will certainly be the case. When all capitals become very large, the rate of profit, and the rate of interest will differ in little or no degree, and every man will receive a revenue proportional to his property or capital. Profits will be reduced to the level of interest, by reason of the regularity of the demand which always exists for the productions of a large capital, and by reason of the steady and inconsiderable expenses of management. The returns from such a capital would be so regular and assured, that this trading capital would be as secure as the capital fixed in houses or improved lands; and it will then happen that a given quantity of capital, that is, a capital which has cost a given quantity of necessaries, will yield the same rate of revenue, whether it be employed as trading capital or not. If all capitals were so large as to render profits and rents equal, the rate of revenue on houses and lands would be at least doubled, and the

common rate of interest would probably be ten
per cent. The landholders and lawgivers of
England might enjoy all these private and public advantages, if they would give themselves the
trouble of repealing the impolitic laws which
chain down capital. It is extremely probable
that if capital were set free and well guarded by
simple laws of property, all the agricultural capitals in England would gradually and rapidly
unite themselves into one great capital, of which
the present landed proprietors would be the principal shareholders. In a similar manner, the
capitals in each trade would become larger and
larger, until they collected themselves into large
single capitals. When the labour employed in
the different arts has been collected into very
large distinct capitals, all these distinct capitals
will probably be united under one government or
head.

The quality of the poorest soils in cultivation
is a good index of the rate of profit or revenue
from capital : in a nation where the best soils
only are cultivated, profits are high ; when the
poorest soils are cultivated, profits are low. The
poorest land in cultivation pays no rent, and perhaps no tithes : the whole produce of such land
will be distributed among two classes of people,
labourers and capitalists. It may be fairly as-

sumed, that nine pounds of corn a-day, together
with a sufficiency of raw materials of clothing, are
enough for the consumption of the labourer and
his family : and that one pound of corn more
a-day for each agricultural labourer is sufficient to
enable him to maintain as much manufacturing
labour as is necessary to prepare the raw materials, corn, flax, and wool, for his consumption.
That is, neglecting the raw materials of clothing
as inconsiderable, ten pounds of corn a-day represents the necessary maintenance of an agricultural
labourer.   The maintenance of a horse may be
estimated at half that of a man and his family ;
the quality of the food which the horse consumes
being such, that he may be maintained by the
same labour, which produces five pounds of corn
a-day.   Fifteen pounds of wheat a-day, or about
twelve quarters a-year, will then represent the
maintenance, and consequently the labour of a
man and horse on the farm for a year, on the
supposition of there being no profits.   Hence,
knowing the gross produce of a farm which pays
no rent nor tithes, we may discover what part of
the produce is paid as revenue, if we also know
what quantity of agricultural labour has been bestowed thereon : the excess of the whole produce
above twelve quarters of corn for every man and
horse employed, is consumed as revenue.   In

England it will probably be found, that half the produce of the poorest land is consumed as revenue. This revenue of half the produce of the land is swallowed up, first by the farmer's taking the ordinary rate of profit on the money expended, then by the house proprietor as rent for the labourer's cottages, then by the profits of the baker, linen-draper, and others, who supply the labourers with necessaries. As the common rate of profit diminishes, inferior soils will be brought into cultivation.

There is a natural tendency in all capitals to undersell one another, that is, to diminish their rates of profit. The cause of this tendency is this:—a capitalist may, by diminishing the price of his goods and consequently his rate of profit, so increase the quantity of goods sold, that his whole absolute profit will be increased. The absolute profit of a trader is represented by the quantity of goods sold, multiplied by the rate of profit obtained: most traders find, that this absolute profit may be increased, by diminishing the rate of profit. When by the liberating of capital, the average amount of capitals shall have so increased, that there be no distinction between profits and interests of capital: the same causes will act in effecting the continual reduction of the interest of capital, which are now acting on the profits of capital. In England, if by reduction of profits to the level of interest of capital, the general rate of interest were increased to ten per cent. (as it most probably would be) then those possessing capital would be continually endeavouring to undersell one another, which would have the effect of diminishing the general rate of interest. When the rate of interest has fallen to nine per cent., a great quantity of poor lands will be taken into cultivation, because they will yield more than nine per cent., on the necessaries expended on the labourers. As the rate of interest diminishes, lands of still inferior quality will be taken into cultivation; until at last, when the rate of interest becomes almost nothing, all lands will be cultivated, which are barely sufficient to maintain the labour employed on them. Such is the natural termination of things if they were to continue in their present course; population would be immoderately increased, and nearly all people would be reduced to the condition of day-labourers on necessaries. Such an extreme is by no means desirable, chiefly on this account,—that the absolute power of the people of a given territory, does not increase proportionally to the increase of the population, but in a much lower ratio. The absolute power of a given country varies directly as the number of people, and inversely as the labour required to provide necessaries for each person. Now the chief necessary is corn or other food, and every one knows that a given space of land will not yield a certain increased quantity of corn, without a considerably greater than a proportional increase of labour. The population of a country will have reached its proper number, when the product of the whole number of the population, multiplied by the time each person has to spare, after he has produced the quantity of corn he requires, is the greatest.

CHAPTER VIII.

Paper and Gold Money.

THE invention of money originated in the saving of labour effected by the " Division of Labour." No people could exist any considerable number of years without discovering the advantages arising from the division of labour. The bartering of one article for another is the first effect of this principle : but barter, going no farther than the exchange of the produce of one man's industry for that of another, or at least very little farther, will occasion a very inconsiderable division of labour. The invention of gold or silver money, gave rise to the exchange of large quantities of commodities for one another, or to the interchange of the products of the industry of bodies of men; the division of labour in consequence rapidly advanced. But gold being a commodity which costs much labour, and the demand for gold or the dearness of gold, increasing with the division of labour or with the magnitude of products exchanged, the increased price of gold will materially obstruct any increase in the division of labour. As the division of labour increases, the quantity of gold, the medium of exchange, must also increase; the people, in order to procure gold, must export necessaries; and since they receive the luxury gold in exchange, they will probably impoverish themselves as much by importing gold, as they have enriched themselves by dividing labour. The invention of paper money remedied this evil by substituting a medium of exchange costing nothing, for another medium which costs, perhaps, the tenth or twentieth part of the labour, which the commodities annually exchanged, cost. The superiority of paper over gold money is as great as the superiority of gold money over the barter system.

I shall now proceed to explain more particularly the manner in which a nation, using gold money, is prevented from increasing the division of labour, and whose progress in the arts is consequently retarded. I would here remind my readers of an observation before made,—that the quantity of commodities, both necessaries and luxuries, consumed by a certain considerable population in any given time, is subject to very little variation. Corn is the only article of consumption I shall here consider : what will be said of corn, is applicable to all other articles of consumption. Quantities of gold and corn of equal exchangeable value, may here be considered as having cost the same degree of labour : thus a piece of gold, which will exchange for as much corn as a man consumes every day, may be supposed to have cost as much labour as the corn. The measuring of corn by gold, will then be nothing more than measuring the effect of one kind of labour, by the effect of a given quantity of another kind of labour ; it will be measuring labour by a given quantity of labour, which may be called a standard. Now a man may have the quantity of corn he consumes, distributed to him daily, weekly, monthly, or at any other period, by means of a piece of gold which cost as much labour as his daily, weekly, monthly, or other periodical consumption of corn. If he be paid weekly, seven times as much gold would be required as to pay him daily : four times as much gold would be required to pay him monthly as weekly. The measuring out of corn weekly to a man, when it can be done daily, is precisely the same as if a man who might measure a certain distance by a foot rule, should measure it by a seven foot rule, which costs him seven times as much as the foot rule. A great deal of the labour of measuring will be saved by this increased length of the standard; but this labour may be more or less than compensated, by the increased expense of the rule. The agriculturist will save a great deal of labour by delivering his corn weekly instead of daily; but the gold required will be seven times greater in the former, than in the latter case.

Before the labour of distributing corn becomes divided, the people will be divided into two classes, viz. one class growing, grinding, and selling corn, the other class being the consumers. The first class will probably pay the consumers at the end of one week, sufficient gold to provide them with corn for the following week: and at the end of that week the first class will have received back all the gold they paid to the consumers the preceding week. The gold current among this people will then represent a week's consumption of corn. Suppose now, the people to be divided into three classes, one of corn-growers, another of flour-sellers, and another of consumers, and suppose as before, the payments to the consumers made weekly. The flour-sellers being numerous, and the same consumers not always purchasing of the same flour-seller, the demand for flour will be so inconstant, that each flour-seller will be compelled to keep by him at all times, at least a quantity equal to his average weekly sale. The corngrowers will not be inclined to sell at less than weekly intervals, neither will the flour-sellers be inclined to buy more than once a-week. The consequence will be, that the flour-sellers will be daily receiving money of the consumers; but they will not make any new purchases before their receipts amount to the average weekly consumption. The class of corn-growers therefore, at the end of a week, can only have received the half of the quantity of gold which they were accustomed to receive, when they were flour-sellers also ; consequently, the gold currency must be increased by half as much as it was before, in order to enable the corn-growers to pay the consumers the same money wages as before. But gold cannot easily be procured; the gold currency cannot be increased by the half, without much labour: in order to obtain this gold, the people must export the necessaries represented by half their currency. The people will gain very little more by dividing la-

PAPER AND GOLD MONEY.   139

bour, than they will lose by exporting their necessaries.   When after some time, a given quantity
of gold represents the same quantity of necessaries
among this people, as among the neighbouring
nations, the farther influx of gold and efflux of
necessaries will cease, and this people will have an
advantage over other nations, on account of its
greater division of labour.   Suppose now a class
of corn-factors and a class of millers to rise up
between the corn-growers and flour-sellers ; each
class will then have the gold which represents
half a week's consumption of corn locked up in its
possession : and in order that the consumers may
receive weekly the same amount of gold, the currency must become two and a half times as great.
Before the currency can be increased to this required amount, there must exist a great demand
for gold, and much corn must be given in exchange
for the gold.   In a country having a gold currency only, as the division of labour increases, the
demand for, and the price of gold increases : what
is saved by dividing labour is lost by exporting
necessaries.   A gold currency is one of the greatest antagonists to the progress of the most important of principles, the division of labour.

The effect of many traders intervening between
the consumer and producer of corn, is to diminish
the rapidity with which money returns from the

consumer to the producer : as the number of trades increases, the rapidity of the circulation decreases. The round which money to be exchanged for corn goes, is this—first, from the corn-grower to the consumer, then from the consumer to the flour-seller, then to the miller, then to the corn-factors, and then back to the corn-grower again. If the money paid to the consumer be retained a week by the flour-seller, a week by the miller, and a week by the corn-factor ; then a four-times greater gold currency would be required to keep the gold price of corn, the same as it was before any traders intervened between the producer and consumer of corn. The circulation of money might, however, by means of a banking system be so accelerated, that the corn-grower may have his money returned as soon as it would have been had there been no corn-factors, millers, or flour-sellers. By means of a bank, the flour-seller might, as soon as he received money from the consumer, pay it to the miller, who might at the same time pay it to the corn-factor, who might pay it to the corn-grower. Although none of the banking systems do so much as this, yet they all tend to increase the rapidity of the circulation, and thus economize the quantity of the circulating medium. In a country which has no outlet for its gold, a banking system which should double the velocity of money, would have the effect of doubling the gold price of corn, or of making gold compared with corn twice as cheap. In the same manner, the quantity of paper money in a country remaining constant, by doubling the rapidity of circulation, the paper money price of corn, would become doubled, or paper money would become twice as cheap. The quantity of money remaining constant,,the money prices are proportional to the rapidity of circulation.

The invention of paper money removed the obstacle which gold presented to the progress of the "division of labour." As the division of labour increases, the quantity of the circulating medium must increase; but a gold currency cannot be increased without great labour; to increase a paper currency costs little or no labour. In all paper money systems which have yet been invented, a certain quantity, or a certain denomination of this paper money, has been fixed as representing or exchanging for a certain quantity of gold or silver. This is by no means indispensable in a paper system; the only useful end gained thereby is, the confining of one thing, which may be varied at pleasure, within the limits of the variation of another thing, which cannot be varied at pleasure, and which is not often subject to very great fluctuations. But gold is by no means a fixed standard for either short periods or long periods : by the breaking out of a war there may arise such a demand for gold, that a bit of paper money, which would before command an ounce of gold, will not now command three-fourths of an ounce. Again : in the same nation, a certain denomination of paper money, or the quantity of gold it represents, will not exchange for the half of the quantity of corn at one time, as it would thirty or forty years before, which will probably be the case in England in 1840. The proper measure of value is, a given quantity of corn, and if a given denomination of the paper currency be made to represent a given quantity of corn in ordinary seasons, a given quantity of paper money will at all times represent nearly the same quantity of labour, and be of the same real value. Suppose the paper money to consist of a number of counters of equal value, and suppose it determined that each counter shall be of equal exchangeable value, with a given quantity of corn in ordinary seasons ; and suppose these paper counters to be issued by one bank : if, in an ordinary season, each counter represents more than the quantity of corn fixed on, the bank must issue more counters in order to make each counter represent more nearly the quantity of

corn agreed on : if, on the contrary, a paper
counter should exchange for less than the given
quantity of corn, the number of paper counters
must be diminished.   No individuals, as merchants and others, must be allowed to coin paper
money, or bills, at their pleasure, and thus disturb the currency.   If paper were thus referred
to the standard of corn, it would tend to destroy
the vulgar and hurtful prejudice entertained of
the existence of a necessary connexion between
money and the luxurious commodity called gold.

Every merchant in England is a coiner of paper
money : if the credit of the coining merchant be
very good, his bills will circulate freely and
supply the place of bank notes.   If the number of
bank notes be increased, the merchant's money
will diminish, and reversely.   The trading currency in England consists principally of bills of
exchange; the currency of consumers consists
chiefly of bank notes.   The proportion of the
trading currency to the consumers' currency is,
perhaps, that of five to one.   All the money current among the traders must have been obtained
from the consumers.   If the money be retained
by the traders five times as long as it was by
the consumers, the trading currency will be five
times greater than the consumers' currency.   The
traders do not use the bank notes they receive

from consumers, but they convert them into bills of exchange by means of banks, and the consumers' currency is quickly returned to them again.

CHAPTER IX.

Armies and Navies.

THE art of war is as necessary and useful an art as the art of agriculture. The agriculturist cannot exist without the soldier, any more than the soldier can exist without the agriculturist. No man will expend labour on his land, when he is not assured that he will reap the produce of this labour. In a country where the art of war is little known, the cultivator can have no strong assurance of his enjoying the fruits of his labour, since he lies at the mercy of his neighbours who are superior to him in the art of war. The greater the progress made in the art of war, the greater is the assurance that the agriculturist will reap the fruits of his labour ; and the greater the security to the agriculturist, the more labour will be bestowed on land, and the more rapid will be the progress of the art of agriculture. A nation which is inferior to others in the art of war, will also be inferior to other nations in the art of agriculture. Not agriculture alone, but all other useful arts are dependent on the art of war. The present greatness of England may be traced up to the national security, which it has derived from its superiority over other nations in the art of war.

The art of war is divided into several arts: there is the art of the soldier and sailor; there is the art of ship-building; the art of fortification; the art of making cannon, musquets, gunpowder, and other arts. What has been said of agricultural and other capital applies equally to a war capital. A war capital, like other capitals, consists of the labour fixed in machinery, and of current practised labour. The capital employed in some of the arts of war consists principally of machinery; the capital employed in the arts of the soldier and sailor consists chiefly of current labour, engaged in the wielding of the productions of the other arts of war. A war capital, like other capitals, cannot be suddenly increased without great difficulty: the current labour employed in the manufacture of machinery must be increased, and the current labour managing this machinery and its productions must be increased; that is to say, there must be an increase of labourers in all the arts of war. But labourers in the arts of war, like labourers in the arts of peace, cannot be formed suddenly : two or three years must probably be expended on teaching a man the art of a soldier, or sailor, or ship-builder, or other art of war. Our attention will now be confined more particularly to the current labour engaged in the arts of a soldier and sailor.

The military and naval arts each divide themselves into two arts ; the arts of the private soldier and sailor, and the arts of the officers who direct the movements of the simple soldiers and sailors. The art of the private soldier consists in the performance of certain evolutions with steadiness and regularity, and at different paces, or with different degrees of velocity ; and in the management of his musquet. The qualifications of an able sailor are comprised in these three simple operations, to hand, to reef, and steer. The sailor's art is so much more simple than that of the soldier, that no reasonable doubt can be entertained of the possibility of forming a good sailor in much less time than is required to form a good soldier. The common prejudice, that the art of a soldier may be learnt in less time than any other art, has arisen from the soldier's receiving more systematic and regular instruction than any other kind of labourer ; in consequence of which, the soldier sooner becomes a proficient in his art. The common prejudice that many

years are required to form a good sailor, has
arisen from the sailors receiving less systematic
and regular instruction than the labourers in any
other art. The progress of a sailor in his art,
is left almost entirely to chance. Let a man be
made to practise handing, reefing, and steering,
for three or four hours every day, at the end of
one year he will undoubtedly become a better
seaman than he could have become a soldier in
the same time.

The art of the naval officer is extremely simple. It consists in the application to practice of
one or two of the simplest hydrostatical principles.
An admiral, or a leader of many ships, can hardly be said to exercise any art at all. A line of
ships or sea-batteries, cannot be manœuvred with
any better prospect of success than a line of land
batteries on a plain. Each land battery will endeavour to place itself so as to take its adversary
in flank ; but the enemy can meet this movement
by a corresponding movement. Two land batteries may place themselves, one on each side of
an enemy's battery ; but the enemy will meet
this manœuvre by placing another battery opposite one of these two batteries. A battle between
two fleets, like a battle between two lines of guns
on land on a plain, will always reduce itself to a
battle of cannon against cannon. The cannon

which are most numerous, or are best worked, will carry the day. The success of the manœuvre of breaking the enemy's line, is wholly to be attributed to the passiveness of the enemy; if the manœuvre be ever again tried, the result will probably be different.

But the art of directing the movement of soldiers is by no means simple. If two equal armies be opposed to each other on a plain, the object of the art of each general will be the attack of a certain position, or part of the enemy's forces, with a superior force. In order that one general may bring a greater force to bear on one point than his enemy, he must weaken himself in some other point: before increasing his force on one point, he must take care that his weak point is far enough removed from the enemy, that, in case of attack, he may be able to succour it in time. The general who brings his strong point near the weak point of the enemy, and has his weak point sufficiently distant from the strong point of the enemy, is pretty secure of victory. The art of manœuvring forces on a plain will be found to resolve itself into a good and rapid perception of distance; these distances being measured, in the general's mind, by the time a body of soldiers could march over them. The general who has the best perception of distance will probably obtain the victory. When the ground is unequal, the art of a general consists in the perception, at a glance, of the advantages or disadvantages of a certain position. A good general will perceive, at a glance, what number of men are sufficient to dislodge a given number of men from a certain piece of ground. When a general has settled in his mind the value of each piece of ground, he will proceed very nearly as he would in a plain, regulating the concentration of his forces by the comparison of distances. The art of a general officer will thus be resolved into a quick and correct perception of distances, and of the nature of different pieces of ground. The combinations of distances and kinds of grounds are innumerable; the power of seizing and comprehending these combinations with rapidity, can only result from long habit joined to a good understanding : the possession of this power constitutes a good general.

The movement of a navy from one end of the world to the other, is very little more expensive, or costs very little more labour, than its maintenance on its own shores; but it is far otherwise in the movement of an army. When soldiers are spread in small bodies over a country, their maintenance costs little more labour than the maintenance of ordinary labourers; but when soldiers are moved in large masses, the labour required to maintain their efficiency becomes very great, on account of the distance it is necessary to transport their food, arms, and ammunition. The horses and men composing a marching army are all animals of burthen; if they should transfer their burthens to the backs of the horses and men of the country through which they pass, the army might march twice as rapidly as it could when they bore their own burthens. It is questionable, whether the modern customs, of sparing the labour of the horses and men of conquered provinces, and of feeding prisoners of war without exacting any labour in return, is not an over-refinement in the system of warfare.

I have shown, when treating of the " Size of Towns," that in a given country, the labour required to supply each soldier with food increases with the number of soldiers, and is proportional to the square root of the number composing the army. Thus the labour required to supply with food each individual of an army of 4000 men, will be twice as great as the labour required to supply with food each man of an army of 1000. There being two equal armies in different countries, the labour required to subsist the army in the more thinly peopled country will be the greater; for the means of subsistence are in all countries proportional to the population; and in general the people, and consequently their food, are equally distributed over the surface of the country. A nation which is peopled only at the rate of ten to every square mile, will have twenty times less food spread over a given space of ground, than another nation whose population is 200 to every square mile; and a given army must expend twenty times as much labour in collecting its food from the former as from the latter country. The labour required to subsist each soldier of an army, varies directly as the square root of the number of soldiers in the army, and inversely, as the number of people to each square mile of the invaded country.

I shall now endeavour to approximate to the proper proportion of the population which ought to be taught the arts of the soldier and sailor. If the demand for soldiers and sailors were as regular as the demand for labourers in other arts, the best method which could be adopted would undoubtedly be, to attach soldiers and sailors to the service in which they have entered, for the greater part of their lives. A given number of soldiers, who have been practising their art for ten or twenty years, will be stronger than the same number of soldiers who have practised only two or three years. If a nation always required the same number of standing forces, the men, like the labourers in any other art, will be most efficient if they serve for life, and should therefore be attached permanently to the service. But it frequently happens that a nation's existence depends on the power of suddenly doubling or trebling the efficiency of their standing forces: now this cannot be performed suddenly, unless a considerable portion of the population have been taught the art of the soldier, or have served two or three years. It may be assumed, that a country such as Britain, with a population of 20,000,000, would be perfectly secure from foreign invasion, if it could bring into action at any time 600,000 well disciplined forces; that is to say, a nation for its security should at all times be able to bring into the field well-disciplined forces, equal in number to the thirty-third part of its entire population, or to the seventh part of the population of the military age and sex.

Three years may be considered sufficient for the formation of a good soldier or sailor. Recruits may be taken at the age of nineteen, and discharged as good soldiers and sailors, at the age of twenty-two. Now the males of nineteen form about the 120th part of a population, slowly increasing. If, then, one male be taken

out of every four of the age of nineteen, in
sixteen years the numbers who have learnt the
arts of the soldier and sailor, will form the thirty-
third part of the population nearly, which proportion I have supposed necessary for the national
security. The standing army and navy will consist of the males serving between the ages of nineteen and twenty-two, and will be equal to the
160th part of the population. In order that this
standing force may suddenly be increased to the
thirty-third part of the population, every man
who has been in the service must be subject to a
recall until he has attained his thirty-fifth year.
A considerable proportion of the best officers and
men should be attached permanently to the service, for the better advancement and progress of
the art of war.

CHAPTER X.

Taxation.

THE proper object of taxation is, to increase
the national power,—by diminishing the labour
employed on luxuries, and adding to the labour
engaged in the production of necessaries, or wealth.
All people are maintained by necessaries only ; if

a man lives and consumes necessaries without contributing any labour to the replacement of the necessaries he consumes; then are these necessaries lost to the nation to which he belongs. In England only one-third of the population are engaged in the production of necessaries; the remaining two-thirds of the population consume their proportion of necessaries without contributing to the replacing of these necessaries. Of this useless population, about one half is employed in the production of luxuries for the consumption of the other half; the reason why the former half labours for the latter half of this useless population, is, that the necessaries of the former half are at the disposal, by means of money, of the latter half. If a man can get the command of a certain quantity of necessaries, he may rely on commanding the labour of as many men as his necessaries will maintain. A good government will, by means of taxation, get the command of a large portion of the necessaries heretofore expended on the maintenance of useless labourers on luxuries, and then apply the labour which these necessaries command, to the production of necessaries.

The only useful kind of taxation hitherto practised, is that whereby labour is taken from luxuries, and added to the labour engaged in one necessary only, viz. — the art of war. If the labourers in the art of agriculture, were increased by the diminishing of the number of useless labourers, the national power would probably be as much increased, as it would have been if these additional labourers had been employed in the arts of war. With respect to the taxes imposed for the purpose of paying the interest of national debts, or the incomes of government pensioners, they do not at all affect the national strength or power. Such taxes do nothing more, than transfer from one indifferent person to another, a certain quantity of useless labour on luxuries. It is of no national importance which of two persons consumes the greatest portion of a given quantity of luxuries; but the national power is greatly concerned, in respect of the proportion of necessaries expended on useful labourers, and on useless labourers. A national debt is usually contracted in this way—the whole class of revenue-holders, are unwilling to transfer, each man according to his income, the quantity of labour required for the national service; they prefer borrowing the useless labourers of certain revenue-holders, who are willing to lend them, on condition of receiving a high rate of interest. A national debt is of the same nature as a private debt; a man, rather than pay down a large sum, is content to pay a small sum annually as interest. A national debt differs from a private debt only in this,—that national creditors are also in part national debtors.

The average quantity of commodities consumed by each English individual, has been shown to be represented by 10*l*. a year; of which 5*l*. represent necessaries, and 5*l*. represent luxuries. But it is the custom to consider that part of a man's income as his own, which he is compelled to pay in the form of rent and taxes : this is improperly included in a man's income, for he is obliged to yield the commodities this part of his income commands, to another. If people's incomes be estimated after this fashion, it is probable that 15*l*. a year each individual, or 75*l*. a-year each family, will represent the nominal amount of income of the English people.

If the whole of a national revenue, were raised by means of an income-tax only, there would be this attendant evil,—that every man would be at perfect liberty, in the disposal of his spare income, and he would not maintain those labourers on luxuries who are least useless, but those who produce him most pleasure. But no system of taxation has yet been practised, which was founded on the principle of proportioning the tax on a luxury to the low degree of utility of that luxury : on the contrary, in most systems of taxation, the labour which is most useless is generally taxed lower than labour which is less useless. For this reason an income-tax is to be regarded as the most useful of taxes, and all national governments would do well to begin a new system of taxation, by substituting an income-tax, or a tax equivalent to an income-tax, for all other taxes. They might afterwards proceed on the principle of taxing all articles of luxury, in proportion to their indirect degree of utility.

I will now mention a few luxuries which are more or less useless, and which ought to be taxed proportionally to their inutility. Beer and domestic spirituous liquors ought to be subjected to a lighter tax than any other articles of luxury. For the labour employed in the production of beer and malt spirits is chiefly agricultural, and the greater the quantity of labour bestowed on land, the more rapid will be the progress made in the most useful of all arts—the art of agriculture. Moreover, the grain and roots used in these luxuries, may at any time be converted into a necessary, and thus prevent all the evils which might otherwise arise from deficient crops, or from an interruption of foreign commerce. *The English landed and national interest would be very much promoted by the diminution or the repeal of the heavy taxes imposed on malt liquors.* The effect of such a measure would be to increase agricultural capitals, and to diminish several of the useless capitals to be found in towns. Next in indirect utility are the luxuries of fine clothes, wines, foreign spirits, gold, ships for the transport of luxuries, &c., which class of luxuries increase the quantity of labour engaged in the useful manufacturing arts, and consequently tend to improve them. But inasmuch as manufactures are of much less importance than agriculture, these luxuries ought to be taxed much higher than malt liquors. The labour which produces the least indirect utility, is the labour engaged in the building and furnishing of expensive houses, the labour of domestic servants, and the labour of horses for pleasure. This class of luxuries ought to be most severely taxed; the taxes should be so heavy on those articles as to amount almost to a prohibition on their consumption. All the necessaries expended on such luxuries are entirely lost to the nation.

The taxable part of a man's income is that part which is not expended on necessaries: this part amounts in England to about 10*l.* each person. This sum will be expended by the possessor on such luxuries as yield him most pleasure; if malt liquors be dear, and if fine clothes be cheap, he will expend more of his money on clothes, and less of his money on malt liquors, than he would if they were both at their natural price; that is to say, the effect of the increased price of malt liquors will be to diminish the number of agricultural labourers, and to increase the number of manufacturing labourers. It frequently happens, that the produce of a tax on a certain article becomes increased by diminishing the rate of taxation. The reason of this is manifest—the produce of a certain tax is represented by the whole quantity consumed, multiplied by the rate at which it is taxed; the first part of this product increases as the second part diminishes, and reversely. Experience alone can discover when this product is at its maximum. The produce of a tax on a certain article cannot increase without the diminution of the produce of other taxes; the increase of the former may, however, more than compensate for the decrease of the latter. The total produce of all the national taxes on luxuries is greatest, when the average rate of tax on each article consumed, bears the highest proportion to the cost of production. By diminishing the tax on the article most highly taxed, the consumption of this article will, in all probability, be increased, and consequently, the general rate of tax on all articles consumed will be increased, and the total produce of all the taxes be increased.

National taxes affect labourers in little or no degree; for labourers in most countries press closely against the bounds of subsistence; consequently, they will receive as wages no more than the bare necessaries of life. If those national taxes, which are apparently paid by the labourer, were repealed, the class of masters only would reap any advantage from such a repeal, for they would immediately reduce the labourer's wages. In England, not so much as the thirtieth part of the produce of the poorest land in cultivation, is probably paid in the form of national taxes. Agriculture, therefore, the most important of arts, is very little affected by public taxation. The price of English articles of export is enhanced in the slightest degree by the taxes.

Taxation, when applied to the purpose of repressing useless, and encouraging useful labour, is the best and most powerful engine of government. If the labour, which in a nation is usually employed in producing luxuries, were to be employed in the production of necessaries, the power of such a nation, would presently be vastly increased. It is not, however, safe to transfer suddenly a large portion of labour from one department to another : it is better that the transfer should be made gradually. Sudden and important changes are dangerous and insecure : it has frequently happened, that a national convulsion, having failed in the attainment of its object, has only served to rivet the chains of the people more closely. Some popular convulsions, having even attained their object, have done little more than change the people's masters ; and have yielded nothing to compensate the misery which the convulsion must necessarily have occasioned. In order that a nation may be solidly and securely improved, it is necessary that the changes should be wrought gradually, without any violent shocks to the interests or feelings of any individuals. The slow and increasing taxation of luxuries, and the slow and increasing encouragement of the useful arts, appear to be the best means of accomplishing this desirable end.

CHAPTER XI.

Knowledge is Power.

THE cause of all wealth or power is labour.
The cause of national power, is the labour which
is engaged in the production of the necessaries of
life. Of two nations equal as to population, the
most powerful and wealthy nation, is that which
can or does produce the greatest quantity of plain
food, clothing, and lodging, and which can produce
the greatest effect in the arts of war ; which is
to say, that nation is most powerful, of which a
given number of people can produce the greatest
useful effect.   Now the end of an improvement in
any art, is the saving of labour, or the producing
of a greater effect, by a given quantity of labour :
thus, by means of an improvement in the art of
agriculture, a given number of people will produce
a greater quantity of corn than before ; by means
of improvements in the manufacturing arts and
the arts of war, a given quantity of labour produces an increased effect.   The nation most advanced in the useful arts will be able to produce
the greatest useful effect ; or it will be able to
produce the greatest quantity of national riches,

power, or wealth;—that is to say, the knowledge of the useful arts, is power.

The end of almost all useful knowledge is the improvement of the necessary and most useful arts, of agriculture, of war, of clothing, and of lodging. All useful physical sciences, with very few exceptions, are or ought to be pursued with this object in view, on which their utility chiefly depends. Many mental and moral sciences have produced a very considerable effect on the advancement of these useful and necessary arts. An improvement in the useful arts, is generally the consequence, or the precursor, of improved moral and physical sciences. Knowledge in the useful arts, may be regarded as the result or the index of other useful knowledge. It has been found in all ages of the world, that those nations which have most excelled in the knowledge of the useful arts, have also excelled in all other branches of useful knowledge, and reversely, those nations which have made the greatest advances in useful, moral, and physical sciences, have also made the greatest improvements in the useful arts. All useful knowledge is then so inseparably connected with the knowledge of the useful arts, that we may correctly say that " Knowledge is Power."

Experience has proved the truth of the maxim, that Knowledge is Power; this maxim alone,

will be nearly sufficient to account for the events
of all national contests, in all ages of the world
Victory always attends the banners of the nation,
which possesses most knowledge.   Two or three
thousand years ago, the Greeks and Romans were
in possession of the trifling stock of knowledge
then current; they were, in consequence, the most
powerful nations of their time.   In the middle
ages, the Mahometan nations had more knowledge than the Christian nations : for that reason,
the Mahometans were generally victorious.   At
the present time, England and France have so far
outstripped other nations in knowledge, that the
power of any other nation is insignificant when
compared with either of these.   The knowledge
of England, is so far greater than that of France,
that notwithstanding the superior numbers of the
French, the power of England is considerably
greater than that of France.

A tax on knowledge is a tax on power.   Of all
laws, the most injurious to national interests, are
those made to prevent the diffusion of knowledge.
The tax on paper, has perhaps tended more to
diminish the power of England, than all other
taxes taken together.   The rulers of a country
should always bear in mind this truth,—that all
laws against the increase of knowledge, are laws
against the increase of their national power.   A

rising nation having, no laws against knowledge, will rapidly overtake and leave behind her the nation which was once the most powerful.

Luxuries are indications of power : they are the result of misapplied power. If the necessaries or wealth expended on the maintenance of la- bourers on luxuries, were to be expended on la- bourers reproducing necessaries, the power of a nation would be astonishingly increased. Two- thirds of the population of England and about one-half of the French population, do nothing but consume necessaries, and produce luxuries. It is probable, that so much as the tenth part of the labour of this useless population in either country, was never employed in war services, even when these nations were making the most extraordinary exertions. It is a common opinion, that luxuries have produced the downfal of the most powerful empires. Although the opinion be correct, the manner in which the effect is produced, is very little understood. When a nation has advanced far in the useful arts, a large portion of the popu- lation is set free from the labour of producing necessaries. This portion becomes divided into two classes, masters and slaves, or labourers : which latter work up luxuries for the consump- tion of their masters. Now, if the nation's war forces require to be increased, the war labourers must be taken from these labourers on luxuries, and the masters must give up some of the luxuries to which they have been accustomed. The class of masters are the rulers of the land : if the national interest demands a war, their private interest demands peace ; for if they add to the number of war labourers, it must be by diminishing the number of their labourers on luxuries. It is this opposition of private present interest to national future interest, which has been the cause of the downfal of the greatest powers. The class of masters, rather than deprive themselves of a few luxuries, will first submit tamely to slight affronts and aggressions of foreign nations, they will next quietly pass over greater aggressions and so on, until they have lost their martial spirit, and the power of repelling foreign aggressors. It may be observed, that a pure monarchical government has this excellence over a popular government, —that the present interests of the monarch are never opposed to the future interests of the nation.

BOOK THE THIRD.

ON MORAL OR MENTAL FACULTIES AND AFFECTIONS.

CHAPTER I.

Mind, in general.

ANIMALS, in addition to bodies, have some internal principle to which all corporeal impressions are conveyed, which principle is the director of the motions and actions of the body. This principle is called mind. The body of an animal can neither feel nor put itself in motion : the mind alone is the sensitive substance, and the mover of the body. The actions of animals, therefore, are nothing more nor less than moral or mental phenomena : they are the visible effects of certain actions on the substance called Mind. Mind acts, and is acted upon, only by the body to which it is attached ; in animal action, mind is the agent, and body is the passive substance acted upon. But the mind itself cannot act, without having been first acted upon, and no mental impression can be received except by means of some corporeal impression. Mental sensations are caused by impressions of, or on the body, and animal actions are the effect of these sensations. Every bodily impression is connected with its peculiar animal action or moral phenomenon. Most moral, like most physical phenomena, are the result of the combined action of a very small number of simple laws; these combinations being infinitely varied. The general or simple laws which regulate mind, are to be discovered in the same manner as the simple laws to which matter is subject. In the discovery of the laws of matter, we advance from complex particular phenomena to less complex phenomena, until we arrive at a class of phenomena so simple, that the invariably antecedent circumstances or the physical causes, cannot be mistaken. The process by which the mind discovers truth is analytical: when the general laws have been discovered, the explication of particular phenomena is performed by synthesis, or putting together the general laws.

The most simple moral phenomena are those presented to us by the lowest order of brutes. The chief animal motion, or the chief moral phenomenon, is manifestly occasioned by hunger and thirst; the sensation of hunger and thirst, and the action of an animal pursuing food, stand in the relation of cause and effect. The action of an animal endeavouring to escape bodily injury, is a moral phenomenon of which the cause is a simple mental sensation. The sensation of lust is the cause of another kind of phenomenon. The temporary sensation of females having helpless young ones, is the cause of another variety of moral phenomena. These sensations are themselves caused by peculiar states of the body; they may be called internal sensations, or passions. The mind, besides receiving impressions from the body, is also capable of receiving impressions through the body; the impressions made on the mind by external objects, may be called *external sensations;* these sensations are transmitted to the mind by the corporeal organs of sight, smell, *touch*, hearing, and taste. The end of external sensations is the gratification of the internal sensations. All passions, opinions, and other affections of the mind, are the result of combinations formed between external and internal sensations. When an external sensation has been combined with an internal sensation, the resulting sensation is to be regarded as an internal sensation, or passion. The internal sensations, or passions, from which all other passions may be deduced, are very few in number. These simple sensations are hunger and thirst, pain from bodily injury, and lust. These sensations are to be found in every perfect animal, and it is hardly possible to mistake the effects of which these are the causes. I would call these simple internal sensations, primary passions, these being the passions or pains on which all other passions are founded. Secondary passions are formed from the primary, by the operation of the two faculties which are to be found in all orders of minds, viz. *memory, and the associating and compounding principle.*

Memory is a simple faculty of mind, by which it treasures up past sensations ; memory furnishes the raw materials to be worked up into knowledge, by the associating and compounding principle. A good memory is one which retains clear and distinct impressions of all sensations which have been experienced. There are, however, very few memories which retain clear impressions of all kinds of impressions. A memory which excels in the distinctness with which it preserves internal sensations, or sensations not immediately connected with external objects, will probably be found deficient in the preservation of external sensations, and reversely. A memory for internal sensations is generally indicative of an abstracting philosophical mind. A good memory for external sensations, is one which marks accurately the relations of time, space, colour, smell, touch, and taste, which attended any circumstance observed. There are few minds capable of marking accurately all these relations ; there are few minds capable of marking accurately even one of these relations in all its different degrees; a memory which retains distinctly one kind of space, will probably retain very confusedly another kind of space ; in the same manner, a memory which excels in marking one kind of taste, will probably be deficient in the retention of another kind of taste. Although the memory of no animal be perfect, it is very worthy of remark, that every kind of the lower animals, has very nearly reached perfection in that species of memory which is most conducive to its welfare. It is of importance to observe, that memory never acts, except when roused by some primary or secondary passion ; no sensation can be retained which has not been closely connected with some passion. The more violent the passion, and the closer the connexion, the more deeply will the new sensation be imprinted on the memory : sensations distantly connected with weak passions will very soon be effaced. An infant mind retains no sensations which are unconnected with the primary passions ; after the formation of secondary passions, other classes of sensations are treasured up in the memory. The passions are the centres about which all the sensations in the memory collect themselves; if there were no passions, there would be nothing in the memory : about the ruling passion as a centre, will be collected the greatest number of sensations. Among civilized men who do not frequently exercise the primary passions, the sensations in the memory are for the most part engraved there by the secondary passions. Love, sociality, pity, sympathy, revenge, ambition, and a few others, are the secondary passions, which usually engrave sensations in the memories of civilized men.

All minds come into the world endowed with certain innate passions or pains : knowledge consists in the discovery of the objects or remedies of these passions or pains, and in the discovery of the best means of attaining these remedies. Although passions are innate, the remedies for these passions are not *necessarily* innate. An animal, at its birth, may suffer the sensation of thirst; but this animal will probably have no notion that water is the remedy for this sensation : in the same manner, an animal which has not been brought up with animals of its own kind, will suffer the sensation of lust, but will be in ignorance of the object or remedy of this sensation or pas-

sion. Memory alone is insufficient to furnish
an animal with any knowledge which can be useful to it. An animal, by looking into the memory,
might perceive that a past internal sensation,
called thirst, was accompanied by an external
sensation called water, as its remedy; but it
would have no grounds for expecting that a distinct present sensation of thirst could be cured
by a similar remedy. The knowledge of animals
is acquired by that faculty of the mind which I
have called, the associating and compounding
principle, memory furnishes the materials on
which this principle may act. This principle collects and unites together all similar sensations existing in the mind: when two sensations perfectly
resemble each other, the bond of union is so strong
that they can never afterwards be separated; and
the two sensations form one of redoubled force.
When a new sensation enters into the mind, it becomes immediately combined with the sensation
in the memory which most resembles it; and the
animal suffering under the new sensation, endeavours to perform the actions connected in the
mind with the old resembling sensation. For
instance, suppose an animal to feel thirst; this
new sensation will be immediately connected, and
in a great measure confounded with past sensations of thirst; all past sensations of thirst will

be connected with the pursuit of water; so the present sensation will be immediately connected with the pursuit of water. Thus the mind connects every new internal sensation or passion of thirst, with the external sensation called water; that is, the mind discovers or knows that the external sensation, water, is the object or the remedy of the internal sensation or passion of thirst.

I have explained the manner in which animals acquire the knowledge of the external objects which are the remedies of their passions: it now remains to be explained how they acquire the knowledge of the best means of attaining these remedies. This latter knowledge consists in the distinguishing of causes and effects, from the attending adventitious circumstances. Every sensation from which knowledge can be derived, consists of two parts at least, one of which is the effect, the other the cause: but most sensations are made up of a great number of simple sensations. The effect is the chief sensation, and is generally a pain or passion; the cause is one of the accompanying sensations: it is my object to show the process by which the mind separates the cause from the other accompanying sensations. The mind discovers the cause by associating and compounding two or more complex sensations. Of two complex sensations, suppose the chief

sensations, or the effects in each, to be exactly
alike : the associating and compounding principle
will unite these chief sensations together, and form
them into one sensation : the two chains of accompanying sensations will consequently be converted into one chain of sensations. In the two
chains of accompanying sensations, there must
have been, at least, one sensation in the one, similar to a sensation in the other, because the
effects produced are the same : but there may be,
and probably there will be, more than two of the
sensations found to resemble each other. *The*
associating and compounding faculty will add together those of the accompanying sensations
which resemble each other, and the sensations
thus doubled will be connected with the effect
twice as strongly as before : but the sensations
which are not common to the two complex sensations, will evidently have their effect diminished.
Thus, out of two complex sensations will be formed
one abstract sensation or idea, in which the force
of the sensation which is the cause, will be increased. Suppose now a new complex sensation,
having the same chief sensation to enter the mind ;
then this complex sensation will be combined with
the last resulting or abstract sensation, in the same
manner as the two first were compounded ; and
the force of the accompanying sensation, which

is the cause, will be still farther increased. A few more complex sensations of the same kind, compounded in the same manner, will so increase the force of the sensation which is the cause, that the remaining accompanying sensations will be regarded as insignificant and adventitious. Such is the inductive process by which knowledge is acquired, as well by the lowest order of brutes as by the highest order of men.

By way of application and illustration, I will show the manner in which a child or other young animal acquires the knowledge of heights or depths. Suppose a child ignorant of height or depth, to suffer a severe pain by falling into a pit; according to a law of mind already noticed, the pain, and with it the accompanying circumstances, will make a deep impression on the child's mind. The pain, here, is what I have been calling the effect or the chief sensation; the accompanying circumstances, I have been calling accompanying sensations : the child has to discover, which of the accompanying circumstances was the cause of his suffering so much pain. The child will probably avoid the place where he fell, because the objects near that place will suggest the pain he has felt; that is, they will excite fear or dread. If there be another pit in the neighbourhood, he will soon fall into it: the

pain he now feels, will suggest and be compounded
with the similar pain he before felt, and the
circumstances attending the two pains will also
present themselves. Those of the circumstances
attending the two falls, which resemble one
another, will be added together; and thus the
impression they have made on the mind will be
increased; and the connection in the mind
between the pain and these circumstances be
drawn closer. Those of the circumstances which
were not common to both falls, will have their
effect diminished, and will soon be no longer
considered as having any relation to the pain of
the fall. After the child has experienced a few
more falls, one of the circumstances which has
been repeated in every one of the falls, will have
its effect on the mind so increased, as ever after
to be regarded as the invariable antecedent of the
consequent pain : this antecedent or cause will be
found to be a certain shade of light which marks
height or depth.

Secondary passions are formed from the primary
passions, by means of the associating and compounding faculty. Relief from pain or pleasure
is the object pursued by all minds. Now pleasure
always enters the mind in connection with other
sensations. Those sensations which most frequently are found accompanying pleasure, become

inseparably conjoined with pleasure in the mind;
and the pursuit of pleasure, and the pursuit of
these sensations, are not distinguished by the
mind.   For instance, suppose the gratification of
the pain of hunger, or the pleasure of eating, to
have frequently entered the mind in connection
with strength, swiftness, or agility of body, or in
connection with bodily power or excellence; then
will the thirst for bodily power and the thirst
for pleasure become identical in the mind.   A
new passion or pain then arises in the mind, of
which power is the object or remedy.   From the
secondary passions thus formed, other secondary
passions may be formed in the same manner, and
so on, indefinitely.   The thirst for knowledge, or
the thirst for mental power, is a secondary
passion.   All opinions are secondary passions:
opinions which have frequently ministered to the
gratification of the thirst for mental power, of
the thirst for variety, or of other passions, become
strongly united to pleasure, or become strong
passions.   An opinion is a sensation united with
other sensations: a deeply-rooted opinion, or a
strong sensation firmly connected with other
sensations, it is almost impossible wholly to
remove.   Hence the futility of the expectations
entertained of suddenly removing popular prejudices.   Even should a man be convinced by argu-

ment, that his opinions were erroneous; yet he would hardly be able to accomplish the removal of those false opinions.

Knowledge consists in an acquaintance with the chain of causes and effects. The only causes and effects which it concerns minds to know, are those which relate to pleasure or the gratification of the passions. All the passions are intimately connected with one another: a man who, from his superior knowledge of the causes and effects pertaining to a particular passion, carries the gratification of this passion to a high pitch, will probably prevent the gratification of his other passions, in such a manner that his passions cause him more pain than pleasure. A well-regulated mind is one which has the force of all its passions so balanced, that the gratification of one passion never prevents the gratification of another. The passion to which all other passions should be subordinate, is the thirst for justice. Without this passion, the most powerful mind can enjoy no happiness; but with this passion, a man can hardly fail to attain happiness. By the thirst for justice, is to be understood, the passion for seeing every man refrain from inflicting bodily or mental pain on another, without sufficient provocation.

All error, false opinion, or false passion, arises

from mistaking causes and effects. These mistakes do not often arise from a deficiency in the power of the mind. They are usually occasioned, either by a paucity of facts presented to the mind, or by the facts presented to the mind being out of proportion to those occurring in the world. For example, let us take one of the most prevalent errors, viz. that money is happiness. This error arises in the following manner: a man who has been accustomed to have many of his passions gratified by means of money, and who has experienced no other kind of gratifications, will have money and pleasure inseparably united in his mind: such a man will perceive no distinction between the pursuit of money and the pursuit of pleasure. But if this man had participated in a great variety of pleasures, he could never have fallen into this error; for he would have perceived, that the greater number of pleasures, all the more refined and exalted pleasures, are not to be purchased by money. The inordinate love of money may also arise from weakness of mind; some memories being incapable of retaining any thing but external sensations: feelings of pleasure unconnected with some sensible object, as money, make very little impression on some minds. Errors frequently arise from a paucity of facts presented to the mind. When but a small number of complex sensations, having a common effect or chief sensation are presented to the mind, the mind is very liable to mistake which of the accompanying sensations is the cause of this chief sensation. For instance, in the example of a child acquiring the knowledge of heights and depths ; if the child has experienced only two or three falls, he will probably mistake some glaring circumstance which may have chanced to attend the falls, for the cause or the antecedent of the fall. Error may be considered as arising from general inductions, founded on too small a number and variety of particular phenomena.

The primary and secondary passions of mind are pains. Pleasure is the cessation of pain. The forces which move minds are pains. When any passion acts on a mind, the mind is in pain; when the passion ceases to act, or is gratified, the pain ceases ; the action of the mind, occasioned by this cessation of pain, is called pleasure. The greater the violence of a passion, the greater is the pain which urges its gratification, and the greater is the pleasure which attends its gratification : the greater the antecedent pain, the greater the consequent pleasure. If there were no pains there would be no pleasures. A mind cannot enjoy pleasure without being first prepared for the enjoyment, by the pain of want, appetite, or desire.

Hope, or the enjoyment of future pleasure, tends greatly to diminish the pain of a passion : when this hope is very strong, as in religious impressions, the gratification of a passion may be put off to an indefinite period, without much affecting the happiness of the individual. All opinions being passions, the more cultivated a man's mind, the more passions will he have ; and consequently, the greater number of sources of pleasure and pain. Happiness, I imagine, consists in the excitation and gratification of a great number and variety of passions ; the excitation, generally, not being far distant from the gratification, and the passion of bodily pain being very little exercised. According to this definition of happiness, a well regulated, cultivated mind is happier than a well regulated mind having few passions ; this arises from the cultivated mind having more food for the indulgence of his passion for variety than the barren mind.

Man appears to owe his elevation above other animals, chiefly to the faculty of language, or the power of articulating sounds. A collection of men will naturally form a language for themselves; they will gradually advance, from a small number of words associated with the simplest ideas, to a vast number of words representing a great variety of combinations of ideas or sensations. The faculty of language improves mind, by permanently fixing a great number of ideas in the memory. Ideas or sensations existing in the mind quickly fade away, if they are not often recalled : the frequent use of the names of ideas in talking and in reading, preserve these ideas fresh in the memory. The ideas. which the words of a language represent, are in a great measure the instruments of thought : these ideas may be called the national alphabet of thought. The more select these ideas of a language are, and the more simple is the structure of this language, the better thinkers will the people be who use these ideas as their instrument of thought.

What mind or the principle of life may be, we are perfectly ignorant; it may be material, or it may be immaterial ; mind appears to be placed wholly beyond the comprehension of mind. There exist, however, weighty reasons for believing that the operations of the mind are performed by the instrumentality of some matter, which is subject to the same laws as other parts of the bodies of animals ; there are also reasons for believing that the passions of mind have their habitations in material organs. It is a well-known fact, that children strongly resemble their parents in their mental qualities ; their mental resemblance is as strong as their bodily resemblance. The mind of a child, therefore, is compounded of two parts, (the one part proceeding from one parent, the other from the other parent.)   The vigour of the associating and compounding principle of mind decays with the body ; the memory also, and the passions in their decline, keep pace with the decline of vigour in the body.   In old age no new sensation can be associated and compounded with old sensations, and no new sensation can be impressed on the memory.   In the decline of life, the weaker sensations or passions are continually dying away, the most deeply-rooted sensations alone remaining.   The phenomena exhibited in the different stages of the co-existence of the mind and the body, afford us good grounds for believing, that mind, when united to body, uses certain material organs of the containing body, as a mould for its faculties and affections.

It is well known, that every species of plant, and every species of animal body, are capable of indefinite improvement, by means of attentive culture alone ; (the method of improving the species, by propagating from the best varieties only, not being taken advantage of.)   The improvement of an animal body, appears to depend on the different parts of the body being exerted in their due proportion, and to a certain degree.   An animal which exerts a certain limb of his body, more than any other limb, (but not to excess,) will have this limb proportionally stronger and larger than the other limbs of his body. This animal will transmit this increased strength and size of this limb to its offspring. In like manner, the aggregate of the material organs which the mind uses, may be increased in size and strength, and the consequent increased strength of mind be transmitted to posterity. If one of the faculties or affections of mind be exercised more than the other faculties or affections, then will the material organ used by this faculty or affection be increased, and this increased power be transmitted to posterity. The body of the parent animal appears to be the mould in which the body of the young animal is cast. The non-transmission of mutilations is not to be regarded as an exception; because, in mutilations, part of a duly proportioned organ remains; whilst in natural defects a whole disproportioned organ is used as a mould.

What is called instinct, is nothing more than innate faculties or affections of mind, acquired by an animal's series of progenitors. The minds and bodies of animals are capable of adapting themselves to circumstances. Every species of animal is continually acquiring those mental and bodily powers which are most conducive to its welfare. Every species of animals, excepting man, appears to have attained the limits of perfection, with relation to its circumstances. Man alone is far removed from perfection; this imperfection of man arises from the circumstances which relate to man, being capable of infinitely greater variations, than the circumstances of brutes. There are very few good qualities of mind to be found in man, which are not possessed in a superior degree by some kind of brutes. In the first of all virtues, in the innate sense of justice, man is far inferior to the ant and the beaver. A strong ant never oppresses a week ant; but, on the contrary, is always ready to assist it. The sense of justice is so perfect in a society of ants, that an ant knows no distinction between its private interest and the public interest of the society to which it belongs. This is an innate virtue, which I am sorry to say has not yet been attained by any race of men.

This theory of innate ideas furnishes us with one of the strongest arguments *a priori* for the truth of the Christian revelation. The sense of justice, which is of the utmost importance to the happiness of man, is contained in these simple words, " *do unto others as you would they should do unto you.*" The inculcation of this truth alone was well worthy of a divine legation. The omniscient Creator may have perceived, that man unassisted would not have acquired an accurate sense of justice for many thousand years. The supporting of the precept, "do unto others as you would be done unto," by divine testimony, and by the promise of eternal happiness, has probably more improved the innate sense of justice in two thousand years, than it would have been improved in a hundred thousand years, in the ordinary course of nature.   The interruption of the ordinary laws of nature, for the sake of so great a blessing to man, is in perfect accordance with the attribute of infinite benevolence, which we may collect from the works of the Almighty. Moreover, this theory of the mutability of mind enables us to overcome some impediments to the reception of the Mosaic account of the creation. The mental qualities of the different races of men now existing in the world so widely differ from one another, that it is hardly possible for a man believing the immutability of mind, also to believe that all men are descended from the same two parents.   The difference between the mental qualities of the Negro and European cannot be accounted for by propagation from accidental varieties, for experience shows that varieties mutually correct one another, so that a national character suffers little or no change thereby.   If it be granted, that mind, like body, adapts itself to circumstances, the existing difference between the minds and bodies of so many races of men, is no argument against the truth of the Mosaic account of the creation.

The gradual progress of the human mind towards perfection will serve also as an answer to the objection urged by some enemies of Christianity,—that if a divine revelation were necessary, it would have been made before the Christian era, because men stood in as much need of the light of the gospel *before* as *after* the birth of Christ. That this objection is without any foundation is sufficiently apparent, when we consider that the minds of men had not, previous to the Christian era, advanced to such a state of improvement as to be capable of comprehending that divine system of ethics, and those momentous truths, which are revealed in the Christian dispensation. The ancient Jews, for instance, could not have comprehended the Christian revelation ; their Divine legislator, therefore, gave them such laws as were adapted to their stage of the mental progress towards perfection.

CHAPTER II.

Manners, Customs, and Religions.

IF we look around the globe we shall perceive that every nation has a set of manners and customs, and a religion peculiar to itself. The customs, &c. of a certain generation of the people of a certain country are always similar, or very nearly similar, to the customs, &c. of the preceding and succeeding generations; some people might consider this sufficient ground for believing, that a generation generates the opinions in the same manner and at the same time as it generates the bodies of the succeeding generation. National prejudices are in some measure innate; but the manner in which these innate ideas are acquired by parents may be shown. The customs, &c. of European nations very widely differ from the customs, &c. of Asiatic nations; and the customs, &c. of one nation considerably differ from the customs, &c. of another nation which most resemble them. The majority of the population of every country is firmly persuaded, with a conviction very little inferior to that derived from the direct evidence of their senses, that the manners, customs, and religion of every nation but their own are absurd, false, and mischievous. The chances, therefore, against the truth of the customs, &c. of any particular nation are very great.

If customs, manners, and religions, which may be termed national opinions, when erroneous, were harmless, or did not diminish the happiness of nations, they would not here be noticed. But most national opinions are erroneous in a greater or less degree ; and these opinions are of such a nature, that they become interwoven with every opinion which a man can entertain. The consequences are, that a man, into whose mind the national opinions or prejudices are sunk deep, will probably not entertain one single correct or true opinion : a nation, whose opinions are very erroneous, can advance but very slowly in knowledge. The greater number of national opinions or prejudices are errors ; and all errors produce misery. It is the nature of truth to produce good or happiness ; it is the nature of error to produce evil or misery.

I shall now proceed to explain the manner in which national opinions are implanted and perpetuated. It has been already remarked, that all errors arise from general conclusions deduced from too small a number of objects on which the mind may exercise its powers of induction. The laws of mind which compel a man to receive the prejudices of his nation, are precisely the same as those laws which compel him to believe that motion will follow impact. The connection between impact and motion is inferred by inductions from an infinite number and variety of particulars ; the connection between national opinions and truth is inferred by an induction from a small number and variety of particulars.

The following is the manner in which national opinions are first implanted. The people of a nation become divided into two classes, wise and ignorant ; the number of wise bearing a very small proportion to that of the ignorant. The wise men knowing the effects of many causes which are unknown to the ignorant, will predict many events which will be found to be true. The ignorant having found many events to happen of which they can perceive no causes, or at least no other causes or connected antecedent circumstances than the words of the wise, must necessarily connect closely together the words of the wise and the reality of the ideas contained in them ; that is to say, the ignorant must correct the words of the wise with truth. The wise, having acquired this ascendancy over the minds of the ignorant, will make some assertion of the truth or falsity of which the ignorant can have no direct experience ; this assertion or relation

will probably be for the advantage of the wise;
they will probably establish a religion of which
they will make themselves priests. The ignorant cannot fail to believe them ; they will argue,
or rather they will make an induction after this
manner; all the surprising events which have
been foretold by the wise, and which we could
have experienced, we have found to be true ;
therefore all the relations of the wise are true.
The ignorant make no more a false induction
than the man would, who having found in a
dozen cases only, that motion was connected with
impact, should conclude that impact *must* always
be connected with motion. If the ignorant were
to be informed and persuaded that equally wise
men had given quite opposite accounts of things
without or beyond their experience, then their
faith in their own wise men would be shaken, and
they would believe those circumstances only, in
the assertion of which all wise men of their own
and other nations agreed.

I have now to show the manner in which national opinions perpetuate themselves. The perpetuation of national opinions is partly owing to
the same cause which implanted them, the connection which the ignorant have formed between
the words of the wise and truth. There is, however, an additional and a stronger foundation

on which the durability of a national opinion rests. If one man hears another assert the truth of a particular fact, he believes it in some degree; if two or more agree in the same statement, his belief acquires additional strength; if all the people he knows, concur in making the same statement, his belief amounts to nearly as great a certainty as if he had perceived it with his own eyes. The cause of this perfection of belief is, that he has always found, when he has the power of examining it, that whatever all people agree in relating is true: he connects with truth the relation in which all people agree, and he regards them as inseparably connected as any cause and effect with which he is acquainted. If all people agree in relating a fact or circumstance which has passed and cannot be again witnessed; and if all or a great part of these people affirm that they were eye-witnesses of the fact; in this case also the belief amounts to nearly perfect certainty. The cause of the perpetuation of error (and of truth too), is the connecting with truth those statements which all the people of a nation concur in making, and of which no individuals can have direct or indirect experience. The induction is made thus,—in all cases which can be experienced, the relations concurred in by a great number of people have always been true, *therefore* such relations or statements are true in all cases. This conclusion is inevitable, although it be false. The only method by which this conclusion can be shown to be probably false, is an induction, founded on the conflicting opposite relations handed down from generation to generation in other nations, on the same grounds of belief. The elements of truth are scattered abroad in abundance through the world; the difficulty is to collect them together; this can be performed only at the expense of a great deal of mental labour, which few people have to spare. The great and probably the only use of history of present and past nations, is, in the furnishing of materials for an induction, (which will be correct in most cases,) that the present existing customs, &c. of one's own nation, are not better founded than the follies, absurdities, prejudices, &c. of foreign, past, or present nations.

It may be proper to observe, that the remarks which I have made on national opinions, &c. are not applicable to the Christian religion, at least not to the religion drawn from a plain interpretation of the Christian Scriptures, and supported by rational evidence. My remarks, however, do in some measure apply to many of the national religions or sects, which call themselves Christian. That man is not a true Christian who suffers his religious opinions to be dictated to him by the authority of men of power, or by the authority of popular opinion ; religious opinions thus acquired are generally far removed from Christianity. One of the most remarkable distinctions between the Christian and other religions consists in this,—that the Christian Scriptures contain many eternal and most momentous truths, the importance of which to the happiness of man cannot fail to be recognized by every reflecting person. The internal evidence for the truth of Christianity is so overpowering, that a man is in some measure excusable for adopting his nation's creed, without a very careful examination of the external evidences of Christianity, and without examining how far his national creed is agreeable to the straightforward, uncontorted meaning of the Christian Scriptures.

The tyranny of national customs, institutions, and religions, is irresistible. Woe to the man who adopts a foreign religion or foreign custom, or who shows his contempt, by actions, of his nation's religion or customs : such a man, in some countries, would be severely punished by the laws; in other countries, such a man would be turned out of society, and if a dependent, he would be deprived of his patrons, and possibly starve. If a civilized man of Europe were to make the important discovery, that nature did not put a beard on his chin, in order that he might have the trouble of shaving it every morning; if he discovered that a Turk with a beard was as happy as a well-shorn Englishman, the Turk giving himself no trouble in opposing the designs of ever-beneficent nature; if he were to make this grand discovery, could he act agreeably to his discovery? Certainly not. If he be a man of independent income, he must choose between these two evils,— the trouble of shaving his chin every day, and the pain of being shunned by all his equals in rank. If he depend on others for his income, he must choose between these two evils,—the daily shaving of his chin and beggary. If an Englishman were to discover, that a large house did not make a man happier than a small one, and that costly dress did not make a man happier than plain dress or clothing; he could not act correspondently, because all his equals in rank would league together against him. He must choose one of these two evils,—the spending of his money on such things as in themselves afford him no pleasure, or the loss of the society of his equals in rank. He could not reap the benefit of his discovery; that there are few or no luxuries, but mental luxuries; because, by acting as his discovery would direct him, he would be deprived of the chief mental luxuries; viz. those arising from social converse between cultivated minds. Such are the baneful effects of national opinions or prejudices, on personal freedom.

But the pernicious effects of national opinions extend still farther. National opinions or prejudices not only prescribe the manner of living to each individual, but they prescribe what opinions are to be entertained by all the people of a nation; they not only fetter the bodies of individuals, but what is much worse, they enchain the minds of the people. If any one differs from the established national opinions or prejudices, he is prevented from making his opinions public, by the fear of incurring the hatred of his neighbours, and in consequence losing the pleasures of society: if he be a dependent, as nearly all men of cultivated minds are, he will be deterred from publishing his opinions by the fear of losing the means of subsistence. National opinion prescribes laws not in the moral world only, but also in the physical: not content with declaring what causes shall or shall not be connected with happiness, it takes upon itself to prescribe laws to matter, and to decide, for instance, whether the earth shall go round the sun, or the sun round the earth. National opinion is the short cut or the royal road for the discovery of the connection between causes and effects both in the moral and physical worlds.

But national opinion, in nine cases out of ten, declares one thing to be the cause of another thing with which it has not the remotest connection. A man who believes those things to be connected together as causes and effects, which are declared so to be by national opinion, may perhaps not have in his mind one true opinion, which he has not in common with the brutes. Such a man cannot possess any knowledge, that is to say, he will not know what things nature has inseparably joined together in the relation of cause and effect, at least he will know no more causes and effects than is necessary for his bare animal existence. When the opinions or prejudices of a nation are very remote from the truth, this nation will be very ignorant, or will have no knowledge in it. Of two nations, that whose opinions are less remote from truth, will have most knowledge, and consequently will be most powerful. Errors in physics are always conjoined with errors in morals: the same mind which can detect errors in physics, will be able to detect errors in morals, for the mental process by which causes and effects are discovered in morals, is precisely similar to the process by which physical causes and effects are discovered.

Knowledge is power. If my readers will allow me to assume what I shall hereafter show, that " knowledge is happiness," I will prove the startling paradox, that the law of the strongest, or war, is one of the most benevolent institutions of Nature. A nation which has much knowledge is powerful and happy; a nation having little knowledge is weak and unhappy. Beneficent providence has so ordained it, that the powerful are continually bringing the weak under their subjection. When a powerful nation has subdued and occupied a weak nation, it diffuses its own customs, institutions, and opinions among the people of the conquered nation. The consequence will be, that after a few years, the conquerors and conquered will become one nation; and the conquered nation will have exchanged their very erroneous opinions, for the less erroneous opinions of their conquerors. If the conquering should endeavour to keep the conquered nation in perpetual subjection to it, the attempt will be vain, because neither of two nations having equal knowledge or equal power can keep the other in subjection. The conquered nation will thus, at the expense of a short period of trouble, have acquired a permanent addition to its knowledge, power, and happiness; such an addition, which if left undisturbed, it would have been an infinitely longer period in acquiring. The conquered nation will receive knowledge by compulsion, which is the only method by which nations ever make a sudden and considerable advance in knowledge.

CHAPTER III.

Education.

EDUCATION divides itself into two parts ; education of the body and education of the mind. The proper object of bodily education is, the attainment of the greatest possible quantity of health, strength, and dexterity of body. Exercise is the chief instrument whereby health of body is acquired and maintained. With respect to the proper quantity of exercise, we ought to take nature for our guide in this case as well as in every other case : children should be suffered to play neither more nor less than nature inclines them. With respect to the kinds of play, or exercise, to be indulged in, a system of education may interfere with advantage ; such plays and exercises as are most calculated to improve the body will be selected and encouraged. Nature intended that every man should labour for his subsistence ; if the designs of nature were to be fulfilled, every man would be required to practise some art for his subsistence. Every child should be instructed in the practice of some useful art ; a short time, as one hour a-day, would be sufficient for the instruction of children in their future art or oc-

cupation. Children should be inured to sudden
and considerable variations of temperature, in order to guard against the accidents which so frequently arise from the derangement or weakness
of the perspiratory organs. Bodily education
then consists in the selection of such games and
exercises as are most conducive to the health,
strength, and dexterity of the body, in the instruct-
ing of children in the practice of their future art
or occupation, and in accustoming their bodies to
sudden changes of temperature.

Mental education has for its proper object, the
instilling of correct opinions or passions into the
minds of youth. Secondary passions, opinions,
prejudices, sensations, are all of the same nature ;
they are all derived, in the same manner, from
the few primary passions. The mental process
by which passions or opinions are formed, has
been already explained ; it is this—when in one,
two, or more phenomena, two circumstances have
been observed to be conjoined, these circumstances
become linked together in the mind ; if these circumstances have been found to be conjoined in a
great number of instances, the bond which unites
them becomes very strong, and the two circumstances become inseparably linked together in the
mind, as in the relation of cause and effect, or some
similar relation. The circumstances which are

thus united in the mind, have frequently no connection with each other in nature: in order that they may be united in the mind, they must first have been united by nature in some cases; but it does not follow that nature has united them together in all cases as true cause and effect. An induction, founded on an infinite number of phenomena, is perfect truth; the smaller the number of phenomena observed, the greater is the probability that the mind will have linked together as cause and effect, circumstances which have no connection with each other in nature. Error is the linking together of two things in the mind, which are not linked together in nature. The separation of things thus falsely united in the mind, is a work of great labour and difficulty; it has frequently happened that these false bonds have resisted successfully the efforts of the mind in which they have been fixed, and of other minds, to break them. If a man have many things firmly linked together by these false bonds, his case is utterly hopeless; for the breaking of one only of these bonds will occupy a great portion of his life. A good system of education will unite only such things as are united in nature; the grown man will not then have to spend his life in unlearning what he was taught, or in breaking the bonds which were formed in his youthful mind.

All errors have their origin in a general induction from too small a number and variety of
particular phenomena. The erroneous passion,
or opinion, that money is firmly connected with
happiness, arises from an induction of this kind:
money is connected with pleasure in many cases,
therefore money and pleasure stand in the relation of cause and effect in every case. The
belief in popular opinions is thus acquired: what
all people agree in stating has been found true in
very many instances; therefore, what all people
say is always connected with truth. The past
belief, that the sun moved daily round the earth,
arose from an induction of this kind. Apparent
motion has been connected with real motion in
a vast number of cases; therefore, in any new
case, apparent and real motion are connected together. These examples might easily be multiplied. Most errors, however, do not so much
arise from a dearth of phenomena presented by
nature, as from the disproportion in number or
force of the phenomena, in which the same two
things are and are not found together. For example, there are innumerable phenomena, by
which a man may perceive that the apparent
motion of a body is not connected with any real
motion of that body; but there are ten thousand
cases, where apparent motion is connected with

real motion, which occur for one case of apparent motion without real motion : but the connection between apparent and real motion in the mind is formed on these ten thousand cases, and the solitary case produces little or no effect on the mind. Again, in the gratification of the grosser passions, money is usually the instrument used ; but in the gratification of the more refined and more numerous pleasures, money is of no service ; nevertheless, in most minds money and pleasure are connected together as cause and effect, because the grosser passions only can be made objects of contemplation of the vulgar. In a good system of education, the phenomena of rare occurrence in nature, and the phenomena which are often overlooked, will be most frequently presented to the minds of the pupils. If an equal number of phenomena, of equal force, of all classes of phenomena occurring in nature, were presented to the mind, there could be no error.

All knowledge is acquired by induction from particular phenomena. No causes and effects can be connected in the mind by any other method, than an induction founded on the particular phenomena presented by nature. A man may be informed that action and reaction are equal, or that a certain quantity of action is invariably connected with an equal quantity of reaction ;

but this cause and effect can never be firmly linked together in his mind, before he has founded it on an induction from a multitude of particular phenomena. In the infancy and progress of a science, from an induction founded on many particular phenomena, some rather general laws are discovered; from an induction founded on these rather general laws, more general laws are discovered, and so on, until the primary laws of the science are discovered. But as soon as the primary laws are discovered, this natural process of the mind is reversed, and the primary laws are used for the explanation of the less general laws, and the less general laws serve for the explanation of particular natural phenomena. This is the unnatural form in which sciences are put into the hands of beginners. It may be assumed, as an incontrovertible axiom, that whatever is in opposition to nature, is in opposition to truth. This axiom alone, even if we had no confirmation of it in this particular instance, would be a sufficient reason for the rejection of the common prevailing method of teaching the sciences. We should have good ground for believing, that elementary books of science begin with what they ought to end, viz. the general laws.

We have only to appeal to the experience of those who have learned sciences after the ordinary method. I would ask these men, whether they had any clear conception of general laws; or whether the causes and effects linked together by general laws, were linked together in their minds before they had studied the particular propositions from which these general laws had been deduced? The answer must be in the negative; for it is a well known fact, that beginners of a science never have a rooted conviction, or a clear comprehension of the general laws, before they have made considerable advances in the science. Although, in the acquiring of a science, the mind appears to be proceeding synthetically, yet in reality the mind is proceeding analytically, or by the natural process of induction from particular phenomena, which is the only process by which mind is capable of acquiring knowledge.

A science may be regarded as consisting of a series of propositions dependent on one another. These propositions may be divided into three classes. The first class contains the few general or primary laws, on which all the other propositions depend, and from which they may be synthetically deduced. The third class contains the propositions which represent or stand for particular phenomena presented by nature. The second class contains the propositions from which all the propositions of the third class may be synthetically deduced; this class connects together the complex phenomena of nature, and the simple primary laws contained in the first class. In the natural progress of the mind, the knowledge of the third class of propositions precedes that of the second class, and the knowledge of the second class precedes and prepares the way for the knowledge of the first class of propositions or general laws. The plan of treatises on science put into the hands of beginners, should be in conformity with this order of nature. After the pupil has acquired a knowledge of the primary laws, by an induction founded on a great multitude of propositions of the third class, he may then be allowed to proceed by synthesis. A scientific treatise on the analytical plan I have been proposing, would be apparently inferior in simplicity to the treatises on the common synthetic plan ; for the second class of propositions must first be shown to be principles or general laws, and afterwards they are to be resolved into still more general laws. But this inferiority in simplicity is apparent only and not real; for whatever is the order of nature is the most simple to the mind. Were this plan of writing elementary treatises on science to be adopted, it is probable that a science might be acquired in he fourth part of the time now usually required.

There are two ways of becoming acquainted
with the third class of propositions, by means of
words, and by the exhibition of these propositions or phenomena to the senses. The latter
method is infinitely superior to the former, for
what reaches the mind directly through the senses,
makes an inconceivably deeper impression, than
what reaches the mind indirectly by means of
words, that is, by means of ideas combined by
the mind and not by nature.   Since all knowledge is derived by induction from this third
class of propositions, and since the induction
must necessarily be more complete, the more
deeply the particulars on which this induction
is founded are impressed on the mind; it will
follow, that the man of science, who is acquainted
with the third class of propositions experimentally, will be far superior in knowledge to another
man of science who has only a theoretical or
verbal acquaintance with the same propositions.
At the present day, a man of science has only a
theoretical acquaintance with the propositions on
which his science is founded.   So great is the
defect in the present system of instruction, that
men of art are generally superior to men of
science ; and that improvements in the arts, instead of originating in men of science, originate,
in nine cases out of ten, in men employed in the

arts. A man of art, is one who is acquainted
experimentally with propositions of the third class,
but who has no helps for the discovery of the propositions of the second and first classes; such a
man cannot fail to discover by induction many
propositions of the second class, but he is not
likely to advance farther. A man of science, is
generally one who has merely a theoretical acquaintance with the propositions of the three
classes. The man of art acts on nature's principle of induction from sensible phenomena; the
mind of a man of science acts by the unnatural
process of synthesis. The consequences are precisely what might have been expected; it has
always been found, that in a new combination
of circumstances, the man of art will decide instantaneously more correctly what ought to be
done, than a man of science will after long consideration. A man of art bears the same relation to a man of science, that a boy who has
been taught by nature to distinguish heights and
depths, bears to a man who should know nothing
of heights and depths, but by the primary laws
of light and of perspective. Such a man, if turned
out of his study into the country, would be compelled to stop at every shade of light which crosses
his path; he must stop to put together his primary laws in order to discover whether, if he

proceeds, he shall knock his head against a wall, or walk over a precipice : after mature reflection, it is not improbable that he would arrive at a wrong conclusion, by a false step in his synthetical operations. But the boy will move fearless and unhesitatingly, without the least probability of mistaking the heights and depths which are indicated by the varieties of light. A moral philosopher is a man of science; a man of the world belongs to the correspondent art. A man of the world will perceive instantaneously and with certainty what ought to be done in a new combination of circumstances; but a moral philosopher will probably come to a wrong decision, after spending a long time on reflection.

One of the most prevalent and most pernicious errors of the day is, that knowledge is to be instilled into the minds of children, by making them miserable, and by no other means. Even if there were any useful things taught in schools, the mischief would not be at all lessened ; for useful knowledge would then be united with pain in the mind, and the grown up man will acquire an utter aversion to knowledge. The fact has been overlooked, that nature has made a provision for the transmission of knowledge from the highest to the lowest order of men : nature alone is capable of making children not only as wise, but wiser than their parents. The curiosity and ambition of men and children are boundless: knowledge is to be instilled in no other way, than by ministering to the gratification of these powerful passions for variety and for power. Men of knowledge, from the thirst for power, have an irrepressible desire of imparting their knowledge, to those who will listen to them with attention and respect. Men and children, having little knowledge, will not listen with attention to men who possess much knowledge, because their arguments are above their comprehension, and consequently cannot satisfy their curiosity; but ignorant men and children will listen with attention and respect to the opinions of those who are a little wiser than themselves, because they are on a level with their comprehension. There is a gradual and imperceptible descent in knowledge, from the highest order of men, down to the lowest order of children. Where there is a free intercourse, men of the first rank in knowledge will be continually transmitting their knowledge to those of the second rank; those of the second rank, will be transmitting their knowledge to those of the third rank, and so on, down to the rank which comprises the youngest children. We need therefore be under no apprehension, lest our children should not become as wise as ourselves, even if we should give ourselves no trouble about the matter. A good system of education might, however, accelerate the improvement of mind. In a good system, pain will never be used as a stimulant. A perfect system of education is that which collects, classifies, and arranges phenomena in such a manner as most to interest the pupil and lead him to make the justest inductions. To childhood, a select number of phenomena should be exhibited, which are founded on little more than the simplest passions: to youth and manhood should be exhibited phenomena, which interest and excite the more complex passions and opinions.

I will now offer a few remarks on the prevailing subject of instruction. If we were to judge from appearances presented by the civilized world, we should conclude, that there was nothing worthy of the name of knowledge, except skill in languages, more especially in the dead languages. I shall confine my attention more particularly to the dead languages; although what I am about to say will be in a great measure applicable to living languages. Language is an instrument of thought: by language, is to be understood the ideas which the words represent, and the manner in which these words are connected together. The better the language, the better thinkers will the people be who use that language. The

ideas which the words of the Greek and Ro-
man languages represent are probably not more
select than the ideas of the English language;
but the method of arrangement and combination
of ideas in English and other modern languages,
is unquestionably superior to the arrangement
in the ancient languages. Even if the dead languages were superior to the English, it would
be no argument for the utility of learning them,
because the using of them as an instrument of
thought is perfectly impracticable to ninety-nine
people out of a hundred. The ancient Greeks
and Romans had made such little advances in
moral and physical sciences, that their authors
do not contain any thing deserving the name of
knowledge, which is not infinitely more soundly
and truly expressed by modern English authors.
If the works in the dead languages contained any
knowledge, it would be perfectly absurd to spend
time in the acquirement of these languages, for the
purpose of getting knowledge, which may be attained equally well from their translations. The
only gain derived from the toil of learning a dead
language, is, the difference between the pleasures
of reading a work of imagination in the language
of the author, and in the language of the translator.
It is questionable even whether this be a gain : it
amounts, at most, to a most insignificant compen-

sation for many years of labour; which years
might have been expended in the acquirement of
such knowledge as would be a source of a perpetual variety of pleasures. Some people urge, as
an argument for the utility of the learning of a
dead language, that many words of a modern
language are derived from words of the dead
language, and that, as a consequence, the words
of the dead language are necessary for the better
understanding of the words of the modern language. Such an argument can be sincerely urged
only by those who are very ignorant of the nature
of language, by those who are ignorant that the
ideas which words represent, and the words themselves, are perpetually varying. If the words of
the English language were traced up to their
roots, their original signification will be found to
be widely different from their present signification: if the words of the English language were
to be confined to their original meaning, the language would degenerate into a language of savages.
By means of dead languages, the *history* of the
words of a modern language may be obtained ;
but the knowledge of the ancient signification of
certain words will afford very little help to the
understanding of the present signification of these
words. A man who knows the roots on which
the words of his language are founded, will pro-

bably be far inferior, in the management of this language, to a man who knows nothing more than the present signification of the words of this language : for in the mind of the former, the present and the past signification of words must be perpetually confounded together.

CHAPTER IV.

Languages.

IT has been already observed, that language, or the power of uttering articulate sounds, is one of the chief causes of the elevation of man above other animals. In the infancy of language, no other words were used but those representing ideas or sensations immediately connected with the primary passions. As man improved, and as the proportion of men relieved from necessary labour increased, new passions were formed, and new ideas connected with those passions entered into men's minds ; the consequence was, that new words were invented for the marking or representing of those ideas. When the secondary passions became very numerous, the words also became very numerous, and a good language was produced. Since the greater part of the secondary passions, being compounded and recompounded from the primary passions, are very complex, the words connected with these passions must represent very complex ideas, or ideas compounded of many simple ideas. The majority of the words of a well-grown language will represent complex ideas. When a word is made to stand for a very complex idea, very few of the people who use that word will understand it as representing the same simple ideas ; this is the cause of the ever-varying character of language : the men whose authority is most respected, will be continually forcing on their hearers or readers their own acceptation of words representing complex ideas, however much this acceptation may be at variance with the original acceptation. This fluctuation in the signification of words of common languages will probably never cease, because of the impracticability of systematizing and defining words, which originated from accidental circumstances. When moral and physical sciences shall have reached, or very nearly reached perfection, a philosophical language may be invented, every word of which may be defined with mathematical accuracy.

The knowledge of the ideas which words represent, like all other knowledge, is acquired by induction. The process by which the names of

simple ideas are acquired is very easy;—a child
or man hears very frequently a certain sound
connected with a certain simple sensation, and
the sound and sensation in consequence become
connected together in the mind. The process by
which complex ideas and their names become
known, is the following,—a child hears a sentence
composed of several names of simple ideas with
which he is acquainted, and of the name of a
complex idea with which he is unacquainted; he
is generally able to perceive the purport of the
speaker, by other indications than the words which
he uses; consequently, by the help of the words
of the sentence which he does know, he cannot
fail to make a close approximation to the signification of the word which he does not know. The
hearing of this word repeated a few times more,
in connection with other known words and actions,
will lead him to the precise complex idea which
the word represents. The acquiring of new complex ideas and their names by reading, is not so
easy, because the meaning of a sentence is not so
readily collected from the context, as it would be
from the action of a speaker. But the process
by which the mind acquires the knowledge of
names in the two cases, will be similar; however,
in the latter case, unknown words must be repeated more frequently, before they can become

known. The knowledge, then, of language is acquired by the frequent hearing of certain words connected with certain sensations. This knowledge is acquired in the same manner as that of cause and effect: if two events happen to be frequently conjoined in nature, they become conjoined in the mind; the more frequently these events have been found conjoined in nature, the more closely do they become attached to each other in the mind. So in language, the more frequently a certain word is found associated with a certain sensation, the more intimately will that word be connected with that sensation, or the better will the name and its idea be known; and if a certain word and sensation be but seldom found in conjunction, the word when again uttered will excite but a vague notion of the sensation, and the sensation will excite but a vague notion of the word, or the word and its idea will be imperfectly known. After a language has been thus acquired, it will be lost again, unless the same means are used for its retention, which were used for its admission into the mind;—that is, the frequent repetition of words in conjunction with their peculiar sensations. This wearing out of the connection between words and their sensations, is precisely of the same nature as the wearing out of the connection formed in the mind between cause and effect.

If a man who has seen two events very frequently conjoined in nature, should no more see
them conjoined, the connection formed between
them in the mind will be gradually erased; in the
same manner, the union between words and their
sensations not often conjoined, will be in the progress of dissolution.

What has just been stated is fully sufficient to
account for the great instability and variety of
languages. The sensations remaining constant,
the sounds or words representing them, are perpetually undergoing alterations by men whose
organs of hearing or speaking are less perfect
than those of others; or by men who are ignorant of the precise sound of a word, from
hearing it seldom repeated. The words remaining constant, the ideas for which they stand,
especially if these ideas be complex, are perpetually varying, by reason of different people
attaching different ideas to the same word. The
invention of writing confined the fluctuation in
the sound of words within very narrow limits.
In the civilized world, the words are constant, the
ideas alone for which the words stand are variable: by means of most authors of reputation
attaching the same ideas to the same words, the
fluctuation in the ideas represented by the same
words, is also confined within narrow limits.
Before the invention of letters, the fluctuation in

languages of every small portion of people, must
have been very considerable : the language used
by one generation, will hardly have been understood by the people of the third generation.
The more extended the use of letters, the more
fixed will a language become.   Without the invention of printing, letters could not have been
very extensively used, and consequently languages
could not have been very permanent.

The arts are very intimately connected with
language.   The arts improve language, and language improves the arts; the invention of letters was
a consequence of the progress of the arts, and the
progress of the arts became much accelerated by the
use of letters.   A farther advance in the arts gave
rise to the invention of printing ; and printing has
caused a yet greater acceleration in the progress
of the arts.   Where language approaches perfection, there also art approaches perfection, and
reciprocally.   If there were no letters in a country, every small district of that country would
use a different dialect or a different language : in
consequence, an improvement made in the arts in
one district, would probably never be communicated to other districts : in such a state of things,
the arts in a large country would be stationary,
or very nearly so.   But when letters became invented, the size of the district using the same
language will be increased, and a greater number

of men in communication with each other will
have their attention directed to the same object :
the improvements made by each man will be
communicated to a great number of other men,
and thus the arts will progress rapidly. In consequence of the invention of printing, a still
greater number of people will be brought to use
the same language, and arts will advance still
more rapidly. *The rapidity with which the arts
improve, is in the direct proportion of the number of
people in communication one with another.* If
every man worked separately, and neither received
nor communicated knowledge of his art ; in that
case, the arts would be stationary, or very nearly
so. If a great number of men receive and impart
knowledge to one another, the progress of the arts
will be very rapid ; for each man will be receiving
the benefits of the improvements made by all
the other men of his art, whilst he himself will
be adding to the common stock of improvements.
A very great number of men can be held in communication with one another, only by means of a
common language ; and a very great number
cannot have a common language, unless they are
accustomed to read a great number of books
written in that language. Since the rapidity of
the progress made in the arts, is proportional to
the number of men in communication with one

another; and since the number of men thus in communication, is generally proportional to the number of people using the same language; it follows, that the progress of the arts will be most rapid, when all the inhabitants of the world use one and the same language.

Because a universal language would be most advantageous to mankind, Providence has laid down laws for the accomplishment of this desirable end. The instrument which Providence uses for this purpose is power, war, or the law of the strongest. A nation which is more powerful than its neighbouring country, will naturally invade, conquer, and spread its own language over the conquered country. When the power of the conquering and of the conquered nations becomes consolidated by means of the use of the same language, customs, and institutions, this compound nation will increase its territories and power, by adding to them the country and the population of surrounding nations. Other powerful nations, in the same manner, will increase their population and power at the expense of the surrounding weaker nations. Thus the average size of nations will be continually increasing, until all the world forms one nation, or at most two nations with two languages.

No two nations can be firmly united under one

sovereignty by any other bond than the unity of
language. Every language is connected with a
set of peculiar customs, institutions, and religion.
Consequently, the same circumstances will not
produce the same effect on two parts of a nation
using different languages. The interests of the
two parts of this nation will apparently clash together; this division of interests will be taken
advantage of by the neighbouring nations, and
the two parts will be wholly separated. Before
the invention of printing, it was next to impossible to unite two nations by a common language.
But since the invention of printing, a conquering
nation may, without much difficulty, force its language on the conquered nation, and with its language, its customs and institutions; and the conquering and conquered nations will soon become
one people, having the same language, customs,
and institutions. The great importance of unity
of language, appears to have been totally overlooked by conquerors, who have generally left the
conquered provinces to acquire the language of
their victors by chance, or rather by the slow natural process by which inferiors learn the language of their superiors. If the chief attention of
the conquering nation were directed to the attainment of unity of language, the conquering
provinces would soon become as firmly united to

the conquering nation as the other provinces of
that nation.

CHAPTER V.

Crimes and Punishments.

THE sense of justice is of infinitely greater
importance to the happiness of man than any
other passion. THE THIRST FOR JUSTICE IS
THE ROOT OF ALL NATIONAL POWER, AND
OF ALL INDIVIDUAL HAPPINESS. The passion
for justice is inculcated in this divine precept, " *do
unto others as you would they should do unto you.*"
An action which is contrary to this precept, is a
crime. The sense of justice is innate in the minds
of all men ; but the innate idea may have been
gradually acquired through a series of progenitors.
The passion for justice is most conducive to the
interests of all men, therefore men cannot fail to
acquire this passion. It may be supposed to have
been acquired in the following manner :—Men
living on seeds and fruits, will acquire the passion
of gregariousness, but they will be subject to no
other law than that of the strongest. On the invention of bows and arrows, if a weak man,
living with a strong man, were to have his bows
and arrows, which cost him so much labour, taken

away from him, by the strong man, he would immediately quit his society and remove far away
from him, to make a new bow and arrows. The
strong man having thus driven away his com-
panion, will begin to feel the pains of solitude;
the weak man will also suffer the pains of solitude, and he would return to the society of the
strong man, if he were not afraid of being deprived of the produce of his labour. This mutual
desire of coming together again, will lead them to
a conference, at which the strong man will promise never again to exert his right of the strongest, or to take away the bows and arrows of the
weak man, if he will come to live with him. The
weak man will gladly accept of these terms, and
the two will again join society. Thus the idea of
justice will be acquired.

The passion for justice is innate in the minds of
all men living in societies: but the force of this innate passion is by no means the same in the minds
of the people of all nations. Among some people,
the sense of justice is connected with a small
number of persons and things; in another nation,
the sense of justice is connected with a larger
number of persons and things. By means of a
good system of education, the innate passion for
justice might be much increased in a few generations. This good system of education consists in

the almost certain award of the *punishment* proportional to a crime. If punishment always immediately followed crime, there would be no crime, and in a few generations there would remain no desire of committing crimes. The innate passion for justice would then become so strong, that no laws, written or oral, would be required for the well-being of society. Men will then have attained that perfection of moral feeling which exists in a society of ants, among which no system of rewards and punishments is necessary to induce each ant to contribute its just proportion to the common fund of labour. The passion for justice appears to be stronger in the English nation, than in any other. This is indicated by the fact, that the relation of the wrongs of an unknown individual, elicits a stronger feeling of indignation from an Englishman, than it does from any other person. Because the passion for justice is stronger in the mind of an Englishman, than in the mind of a man of any other nation, England is more powerful than any other nation. The passion for justice is however very far from being perfect in the mind of an Englishman. There are very few Englishmen who act according to justice, when their apparent private interest is opposed to the interest of an unknown individual. Few men strictly observe the rules of justice, even within the circle of their most intimate acquaintance.

That individuals should observe the rules of justice in their transactions one with another, is of the greatest importance to the national power, and to the happiness of the individuals themselves. If there had been no sense of justice in the mind of man, the human race could never have risen above the level of the monkey race. If the passion for justice had not made some considerable progress, the arts could not have made any advances, and the principle of the " division of labour" could not have been taken advantage of. The source of all national power is the " division of labour ;" commerce, or the exchange of one article for another, is necessarily connected with the " division of labour." If there be no commerce or trade, there can be no " division of labour ;" if the risks and difficulties attending commerce be great, then will the " division of labour" have made very little progress. If the rights of property were not respected and enforced, unless a man was in possession of, or present with, his property, there would be very little commerce, and, consequently, very little " division of labour," and very little national power. In order that the " division of labour" may be great, it is necessary that large amounts of commodities should be pass-

ing and repassing between individuals at a great
distance from one another.   The safe transmission of a commodity to the proper person must
depend on the honesty of a great number of individuals, or on the administration and goodness
of the laws made for the protection of property.
Commerce, and consequently the " division of
labour," and national power, are proportional to
the security of property.   Insecurity of property
affects, in the highest degree, the happiness of
individuals and the power of nations ; *insecurity
of property may be regarded as the cause of all
national poverty, ignorance, and misery.*   Those
nations where property is most secure, have always been found to be the most powerful, and
consequently the wisest of nations ; on the other
hand, those nations are the poorest and most ignorant in which property is least secure.

I will now explain the manner in which security of property acts in another respect on the
national power.   Security of property in land far
exceeds every thing else in importance.   Suppose a man to possess a certain quantity of land,
and a dozen slaves ; and suppose, that in a certain state of security of property he employs six
of the slaves in agriculture and six as menial
servants.   Suppose now the security of property
to become increased, he will probably increase his

agricultural slaves to seven, and diminish his menial servants to five; because he will expect thus
to raise a sufficient excess of agricultural produce
to purchase a new slave at the end of the year.
At the end of two or three years he will possess
seven agricultural and seven menial slaves.   If
the security of property increases still farther, he
will proceed in the same manner until he gets
eight agricultural and eight menial slaves; and
so on.   If, on the other hand, the security of property should be diminished, and if the master
should have the food necessary for the support of
two slaves taken away from him, he must sell
one of his slaves, and he will apply less labour
to his land in the following year.   If the security
of property be farther diminished, his agricultural
slaves and his menial slaves will be farther diminished.   The power of a nation chiefly depends
on its population, and the population is proportional to the number of agricultural labourers, or
to the labour bestowed on land.   Where property
is insecure, very little labour will be bestowed on
land, and the nation will have a thin population
and little power.

The national beneficial effects of security of
property, arise from the confidence with which
people look to the enjoyment of the distant fruits
of present industry.   The nearer this confidence

approaches to certainty, the greater will be the national benefit. If there were no security of property, a man would employ no labour on any subject where the fruits were distant; in such a state of things, a man would expend all the necessaries he commands on the maintenance of menial servants. But if property were secure, a man would diminish from the number of his menial servants, and add them to his agricultural servants; because he relies with confidence on the gathering of the future produce of their labour, and thus increasing his wealth or power. It is a common erroneous notion that national wealth cannot increase rapidly, unless a man is allowed to dispose of his property after death: it is generally imagined, that the power of commanding property after death is absolutely indispensable to the rapid improvement of a nation. The free disposal of property after death is not so great a stimulant of national industry, as the compulsory equal division of property among a man's children. The truth of this must be manifest to every one who will compare the exertions made by the English to improve their property, with the exertions made by the French since their Revolution. I do not say that the French law is more conducive to the production of national wealth or power than the English law; but I assert, that the French law is a greater stimulant to industrious exertion than the English law.

The security of property is probably greater in England than in any other country in the world; yet the security is by no means so perfect as it might be rendered, by the simplifying of the written laws relating to property. In England, there is an abundance of tolerably good laws for the security of property; if these laws were administered at the public expense, there would not be much harm done; but as the expense of administering these laws is borne by the claimants of property, it becomes a very heavy tax on justice. The expense of getting justice is so great, as to produce a very considerable effect on the security of property : such an insecurity is thereby produced, as materially to affect the increase of the national wealth or power. The remedy of this evil is of the simplest kind : it consists in the diminution and simplification of the written laws relating to property, and in determining the rights of property by the principles of justice implanted by nature in every man's breast. The rights of property would be most fully secured, and at the most trifling expense, by the establishment of a court of judicature in every town; the members of this court to be chosen annually by the inhabitants of the town. This court should be empowered to compel the immediate payment of all justly-claimed debts, and to inflict penalties or punishments on all violators of the rights of property, whether by fraudulent practices or by common stealing. In case the evidence on both sides of a question be equal, the court ought manifestly to divide the disputed property equally between the claimants, and not (according to the present absurd practice) to give the whole to the party on whose side the evidence preponderates in the slightest possible degree. To prevent all chance of partiality, the proceedings of all town courts should be made public, and a county court should be established for the purpose of correcting any partiality which might appear in the town courts. If such courts were established in every town, and if the united property of companies of men enjoyed as much protection as the property of individuals, England would very rapidly advance to the highest pitch of wealth and power.

Previously to the establishment of such courts, the tenure of property must be simplified. This object might be attained by abolishing the power of entailing property, and by not allowing a man to order, by his will, what second person shall enjoy his property after the death of the first person to whom he has bequeathed it. The possessor of any kind of property should have the same absolute command over it as he would have over a sum of ready money in his possession. When the tenure of property becomes thus simplified, men of the plainest sense will be able to decide most correctly on the rights of property. Every man in this case would be able to make his own will without the assistance of lawyers. That there may be no danger of forged wills, every will should be lodged by the maker in a public office, and placed under seal. A good regulation might be added, of this kind, that possession of property for ten years should confer an indefeasible right of property.

' Honesty is the best policy,' is one of the commonest and truest of maxims. Providence has so ordered it, that no man can injure another without being injured in return : and it generally happens, that the injury returned is greater than the injury inflicted. For example, a trader who uses deception and injures his customers, may derive immediate benefit from his fraud, but this advantage will be much more than compensated by the loss he will sustain, by his former customers refraining from all dealings with him. Again, a man who inflicts an injury on another man, whether by word or deed, not only makes this man his enemy, but he draws on himself the enmity of all other men, who will ever after treat him with distrust, or as an enemy. No man who is accustomed to act unjustly can be treated as a friend by any body. A man who has contracted a habit of acting unjustly, will be making enemies of all men ; a man, in whose mind the principles of justice have taken deep root, will be making friends of all men. Nature has made all men mutually dependent on one another, for pleasure or happiness. A man, to whom all the world are enemies, or a man who has no friends, can have no more pleasures than a wild beast ; a man who has a great number of friends, will enjoy a great number and variety of pleasures. The greater the number of friends a man has, the greater the quantity of happiness which he will enjoy. Honesty or justice is indispensable for the securing of friends, and consequently for the enjoyment of happiness. The man who acts with the greatest honesty or justice, enjoys most happiness. None but a weak, ignorant mind can act with injustice ; for every well-informed mind must perceive, that by an act of injustice it obtains a small present good, at the expense of a great future evil. Ignorance is the cause of injustice. When the veil of ignorance is wholly removed, every man will then perceive that ‘ ho-

nesty is the best policy,' and he will act correspondently.

National justice, or justice between nations, has
no existence, because (in the present imperfect
state of the passion for justice), nations do not find
it to be their interest to act with justice towards
one another.   Nations do not, like men, mutually
depend on each other for happiness.   A nation
separated by enmity from all other nations, is just
as happy as if it were united by peace with all
other nations; but a man separated from all other
men is miserable.   Justice, or the sacrifice of the
law of the strongest, promotes the happiness of
individual men : but (in this age of the world)
men embodied into societies, or nations, receive
little benefit from the sacrifice of their right of the
strongest; consequently, there is little justice between nations.   The rights of nations are the rights
of the strongest.   Nations may league together
for the prevention of the increase of each other's
dominions ; but experience has shown, that the
weaker nations never firmly unite their strength,
in order to prevent the aggrandizement of the
powerful nations.   Almost all national struggles,
have been struggles between two nations only.
The late contest between the allied armies and
France, was very little more than a national

struggle between England and France, the armies which opposed France being maintained by England. It is the interest, and therefore the rule of action, of every nation, to increase its territory, by diminishing the territories of its weaker neighbours, provided, that by so doing it does not provoke the violent hostility of a nation more powerful than itself. France is prevented from annexing Spain and Portugal permanently to its dominions, not by the fear of the united power of the surrounding weaker nations, but by the fear of the superior power of England. The balance of power, or the regulation of the territorial extent of European nations, is now in the hands of England. This balance of power may be lost to England, either by the rapid increase of the knowledge and power of France, or by the more powerful states of Europe dividing among themselves the territory of the weaker states, and thus increasing their power, relative to the power of England.

People of the higher ranks may protect their property from the fraud and violence of themselves and of the lower ranks, by the impositions of penalties or punishments. The criminal codes of most countries are formed chiefly for the protection of the property of the higher ranks from the violence of the lowest rank. Nearly all crimes which are noticed by the laws, are committed by the lowest rank of

people. The number of crimes committed in a
country is generally proportional to the difference
between the common punishment inflicted by the
law, and the ordinary mode of living of the lowest
rank. In England, the common punishment of
crime is hard labour ; but the lowest rank of men,
if they commit no crime, are condemned to perpetual hard labour, with no more luxuries than
they can get in gaol. There is therefore no ade-
quate punishment for crime in England, and consequently crime prevails there to an enormous
extent. The only means by which crime may be
diminished, is by the elevation or improvement of
the condition of the lowest rank of labourers.
This is to be effected by the diminution of the
supply of labourers, or by the diminution of pauperism. Now pauperism is caused by improvident
propagation, which again is caused partly by ignorance, but chiefly by laws directly or indirectly
encouraging marriages. The crimes of the lower
classes may be traced to that rage for legislation,
which violates the natural rights and liberties of
the subject.

CHAPTER VI.

Gregariousness, or Sociality.

THE passion for gregariousness is to be found
in almost all orders of animals, even in animals
of prey.   This passion is innate in all gregarious animals, but it is first acquired by their
series of progenitors.   The thirst for gregariousness is a secondary passion, compounded from
primary and secondary passions.   One of the
first secondary passions formed in an animal's
mind is the love of power, or the love of excellence.   In the earliest infancy of mind, animals love to excel one another only in the gratification of their primary passions; but in the
next stage of the mind's progress, animals love
power for its own sake.   Nature has presented
to the mind power, in connection with pleasure,
in many cases;   and animals have connected
power, or excellence, with pleasure, in all cases.
The pursuit of power is the pursuit of pleasure
with all minds.   With the lower animals, the
passion for power is confined to bodily power, or
excellence; but with man, the passion for power,

in addition to bodily power, embraces the infinite
varieties of mental power.   The passion for power
being thus formed, the passion for gregariousness
becomes immediately formed, for the majority of
the modifications of the passion for power are
dependent for their gratification on the presence
of animals of the same kind.   The mind first
joins power to pleasure, and then society to power
and pleasure.   Thus is formed that constituent
part of the passion for gregariousness which is
dependent on the passion for power.   But there
are two more passions, on which the passion for
gregariousness is founded, viz. the secondary passion of self-love and the primary passion of lust.
These two passions produce their effect in a
somewhat similar manner.   By the operation of
the passion of self-love, an animal acquires a
strong love for its own body ; now it is a law of
nature, that similar things should produce similar
effects on the mind, and that the more closely
any two things resemble each other, the more
closely will their effects on the mind resemble
each other.   As a consequence of this law, an
animal will love most those animals whose bodies
most resemble its own, and it will have a tolerably
firm attachment to all the individuals of its species.   The passion for gregariousness will be ac-

quired in this manner by a series of progenitors, and it will be transmitted to posterity as an innate idea, passion, or sensation.

Sociality, or the collection together of many men, is the foundation on which the culture and improvement of mind rests. If men had been compelled by nature to live as distant from each other as beasts of prey are, their minds would never perhaps have excelled those of beasts of prey. All kinds of gregarious animals are superior to all kinds of solitary animals, or animals of prey; that is, gregarious animals have a greater number of passions than solitary animals, which latter are seldom possessed of any other than the primary passions of mind. Man excels all other kinds of gregarious animals by reason of its exclusive possession of the faculty of language. The love of power, which necessarily arises in the minds of all gregarious animals, is limited in brutes to the love of bodily power; but in man, by means of language, the love of power embraces the infinite varieties of mental power. To the love of mental power may be traced all the progress of the human mind. In the first stages of the progress of the human mind, the passions formed are, the love of excelling in imitation, in ridicule, in description, in anecdote, in wit, in eloquence, and in other things: the last and most important passion formed is the love of excelling, in the abstract, philosophical investigation of causes and effects, or in the love of tracing all physical and moral phenomena up to a few simple phenomena or primary laws. This last mentioned modification of the love of power cannot exist without the other inferior modifications of the love of power. These latter passions furnish the materials, whereon alone the former passion is capable of operating. All the passions which have mental power for their object are mutually dependent on each other: no one of these passions can be improved, or have its limits extended, without the simultaneous improvement of the rest of these passions. But the existence of these passions is dependent on sociality, or on the collecting together of men, and the rapidity with which these passions are improved, is (like the rapidity with which arts improve) proportional to the number of people in communication with each other. Hence it follows, that all the passions for mental power, all the passions which elevate the human race above other races of animals, increase the more rapidly, the more numerous are the individuals collected together forming a society; that is to say, *the increase of knowledge is proportional to the increase of gregariousness or sociality.*

The inventions of writing and printing, have enabled people who cannot congregate together, to intercommunicate their improvements of these passions for mental power. The eminent poet, or orator, discovers and exhibits new combinations of words, by which the passions of the hearers may be better roused : those men who have the love of excelling in imitation, description, or persuasion, will take advantage of these discoveries, and will employ them in the increasing of their power. By means of books, a man may acquire a considerable knowledge of the chain of causes and effects relating to the passions for mental power, without entering much into society.   But this knowledge cannot, without great difficulty, be reduced to practice : such knowledge seldom influences any body but the possessor of it.   As I have before remarked, truths which are collected immediately from the phenomena of nature, make an infinitely deeper impression on the mind, than truths collected at second-hand from verbal propositions.   The closet philosopher collects his knowledge from verbal propositions, the philosophic man of the world from the phenomena immediately presented to him by nature.   The greatest progress may be made in sound knowledge applicable to practice, by means of a *very large society of men, and a small society of choice books.*

The powerful effect of sociality in the removal of ignorance, error, and prejudices, must be manifest to every one who is accustomed to the slightest degree of reflection.   Prejudices are always found to be most inveterate in such people as have the smallest society both of men and books.   The pertinacity with which the most absurdly erroneous opinions are adhered to in the world, is wholly to be attributed to the very confined society to which most people are limited. If societies were so enlarged, that men entertaining widely conflicting opinions could be brought together, these opinions would mutually correct each other, and dogmatism and error would quickly disappear from the world.   The intercourse between two men of any opposite prejudices, generally ends in the loss of each party's prejudices, and in the arrival of the minds of both parties at some intermediate opinion.   The beneficial effect produced on the minds of ignorant or prejudiced persons, by a free intercourse with wiser men, is too obvious to need any particular remark.   What has just been said, is sufficient to show the intimate connection subsisting between extent of society and extent of knowledge.

If the whole sum of pleasure enjoyed by a well cultivated mind during its life, were to be divided into one hundred equal parts, it is probable that ninety-nine of these parts would be social pleasure, or pleasure derived from and shared with other minds. Social pleasures appear to be of a totally distinct character from solitary pleasures : social pleasure is generally attended by a certain indefinable sensation of inward swelling satisfaction or greatness ; solitary pleasure seems chiefly to consist in the cessation of pain. The solitary pleasures common to all animals are those of eating and drinking ; the getting of money is the chief solitary pleasure indulged in by civilized men ; gambling may be reckoned among the solitary pleasures. I would appeal to the gourmand, the solitary drunkard, the miser, and the gambler, and ask them whether the gratification of their favourite passions ever amounts to any thing more than the momentary cessation of pain ? Solitary pleasures depress men to the level of the lowest brutes ; social pleasures elevate men to the level of the gods. There are some pleasures of solitude to which the remarks I have made on solitary pleasures are not applicable ; the pleasures I allude to, are the pleasures arising from reflection on past pleasures, and from new combinations of ideas made by the mind, and not immediately communicated to other minds. These pleasures of solitude can be enjoyed only by such men as are accustomed to the pleasures of society, either of men or books ; the more extensive this society, the greater the degree of pleasure from solitude. The dependency of the pleasures of solitude on the social pleasures, is a sufficient reason for drawing a broad line of distinction between them and other solitary pleasures. The pleasure derived from the reading of books is to be regarded as a social pleasure, books being the medium through which distant minds hold converse and associate with one another ; however, this indirect social pleasure is far inferior to the pleasure derived from the direct and immediate intercourse between two minds. It may be affirmed, with considerable truth, that the happiness enjoyed by a man is proportional to the extent of his society.

The chief of all social pleasures, the pleasure compared with which all other pleasures are insignificant, is friendship, or the pleasures founded thereon. The closer the ties of friendship between two or more individuals, the greater will be the happiness enjoyed by these individuals. Now one of the bonds of friendship is beauty ; and beauty consists of two parts, mental and corporeal beauty. The force with which one man attaches himself

to another is proportional to the number of simple
ideas which enter into his compound idea of
beauty, and to the proportion of the qualities
represented by these simple ideas, perceived in
the man towards whom the attachment is formed.   Friendship increases as the number of ideas
of which beauty is compounded increases.   In an
uncultivated mind, in a mind having few passions
or opinions, the idea of beauty will be compounded of a very small number of simple ideas: in such
a mind, little more than corporeal qualities will
constitute the idea of beauty.   In a well cultivated mind, in a mind having many passions or
opinions, the idea of beauty will be compounded
of a great number of simple ideas ; the idea of
beauty, in such a mind, will be composed of a
vast variety of agreeable qualities both of body
and mind.   The uncultivated mind can have but
few friendships, because there are but a small
number of points of union between his mind and
other minds.   But the ties by which cultivated
minds may attach themselves to one another are
innumerable ; every similar opinion entertained
by two minds is a bond of attachment.   Among
cultivated minds every mind will feel friendships
for a great number of other minds ; but these
friendships will vary in degree, and will be pro-

portional to the quantity of beauty perceived in
in each mind.

The mutual perception of beauty is one of the
bonds of friendship. But there is another bond
of friendship—it is that sympathy which naturally exists between two minds which stand in the
relation of protector and protected. This sympathy takes its rise from the passion for power; the
protected ministers to the gratification of the passion for power of the protector, by his respect and
devotion; in consequence the protector regards
him with affection. The affection of the protected
is of the nature of gratitude, or is a reflection of
the affection of the protector. Most friendships
will be founded on both these bonds, the perception of beauty, and the sympathy just mentioned.
Every individual having a feeble mind or body
will seek to attach itself for protection to an individual possessing a vigorous mind or body. And
every strong individual will seek the attachment
of some weak individual which will not dispute its
claims to either mental or corporeal superiority.
The talents or powers of the body are so conspi-
cuous, that they are seldom estimated either above
or below the truth; there exists, in consequence,
a natural sympathy between all individuals having weak and strong bodies. But with minds

the case is very different; the talents and powers of minds cannot, like those of bodies, be easily measured and compared with each other, so that all the spectators may agree in coming to the same result. Superiority of body can be understood and justly appreciated by all; but mental superiority can be discovered and appreciated correctly by a very small number of persons only. Most minds are incapable of judging correctly of the powers of other minds which entertain opinions widely differing from their own. An inferior mind is incapable of deciding which of two superior minds is the superior. An inferior mind will generally regard that mind which is immediately above its own level as superior to the mind which is much above this level, because the opinions of the latter will be frequently above his comprehension, and at variance with his own opinions. In general, inferior minds entertain mental respect only for that rank of minds which is removed one degree above them. The sympathy dependent on bodily superiority and inferiority frequently unites individuals who differ very much in bodily talents; but the sympathy dependent on mental superiority and inferiority seldom unites those who greatly differ in mental power or talents. The addition of the primary passion of lust to the secondary passion of friendship forms sexual love, which passion is the result and crown work of all other passions.

The happiness which different men enjoy, is generally proportional to the number of people to whom they are attached by the bonds of friendship, and to the strength of these bonds. The degree and number of attachments formed by individuals are in general proportioned to the cultivation which their minds have undergone ; the more the bodies and minds of individuals are improved, the greater quantity of happiness will they enjoy. Without some other mind or minds to sympathise with, it is probable that no mind could receive any positive pleasure. As sympathy, friendship or love increases, happiness increases.

Man is by nature the most gregarious of animals, for the causes of gregariousness are stronger in man than in any other kind of animals. Men must therefore feel the greatest pain when deprived of the society of their species. Nevertheless, in the civilized world, men are separated from each other almost as much as beasts of prey are from necessity. Men are divided into families of parents and children, each family having frequently as little intercourse with other families, as a tigress and her cubs have with other tigresses and their cubs. In some countries there is a freer intercourse than others between individuals of different families; but men in civilized countries, seldom or never congregate in numbers for any considerable time, like other gregarious animals. The natural propensity of man for gregariousness is more checked in England than in any other country; and, for that reason, the English enjoy less happiness than any other people. The inhabitants of every English town are divided into a multitude of different ranks, the people of one rank having no intercourse with the people of any other rank: the individuals of the same rank meet together for a few hours only, during the week, at each others' houses. This excess of non-gregariousness in the English customs, is the cause of the English possessing a greater pride and ferocity of character than any other civilized people. The English character would be still worse than it is, if the want of society of men were not in some degree compensated by the society of books.

The happiness and knowledge of civilized men might be very much increased, by men's obeying the dictates of nature, and associating together like other gregarious animals. Nature has not connected any of the lower animals together by the ties of relationship, nor has it connected man by any such ties, (I except, of course, the passion which attaches females to their helpless young ones.) The mutual attachment generated by a community of interest, has been mistaken for a natural bond. Men may add to their happiness and knowledge by forming themselves into families of eight or twelve friends. These families should be so united together as to allow the greatest freedom of intercourse between individuals of different families, and to favour the occasional collecting together of men in great numbers. The individuals forming a family should not be permanently united to one another, but individuals should be left at liberty to form themselves into new families when they get tired of each other. It might be a good regulation, not to permit the dissolution of a family before it has endured the space of one year.

CHAPTER VII.

Knowledge is Happiness.

WE have already seen that " knowledge is power ;" it now remains to be shown that knowledge is happiness. The chief cause of power is the knowledge of the physical arts and sciences; the chief cause of happiness is the knowledge of the moral or mental arts and sciences. Physical knowledge is the cause of power, moral knowledge is the cause of happiness. Physical and moral knowledge are however very intimately connected together; physical knowledge cannot be increased without being immediately followed by an increase of moral knowledge, and reversely. The process by which the mind acquires the knowledge of externals or physics, is precisely similar to the process by which it acquires the knowledge of internals or morals : this process may be called induction. It is a process by which the mind involuntarily collects general laws from a multitude of particular phenomena presented to it. By means of words, a vast number of physical phenomena may be accurately expressed; these phenomena, when thus collected and treasured up, furnish the materials for the discovery of general laws ; and these general laws when discovered, lead to the discovery of still more general laws. But moral phenomena are in most cases so complicated, that it is impossible for words to express all their circumstances, with any considerable accuracy ; the consequence is, that there is not a sufficient number of particular moral phenomena treasured up in books, to furnish materials for a correct induction of the primary laws of mind. In the acquisition of moral knowledge, men must trust principally to their own experience, or to their own industry in collecting and examining moral phenomena : in the acquisition of physical knowledge men may securely trust to the observations and inductions experienced and recorded by other men. A man, for his advance in moral knowledge, depends on his own individual exertions ; for his physical knowledge he has the assistance of a vast number of men, predecessors and contemporaries.

When a man has long been exercising his mind, in making inductions from physical phenomena, his power of induction, or his power of seizing the general law which connects together a certain number of particular phenomena, will be increased. The mind of such a man will be well prepared for examining and making correct inductions from moral phenomena presented to him ; but it generally happens, that a man who has

thus increased his power of mind, will have treasured up very few moral phenomena, and consequently will have no materials for the building up
of a moral science. Such a mind will, however,
be able so to arrange these scanty materials as to
form a much better connected system, or a much
better science, than could be formed by a mind
which has treasured up a great multitude of moral
phenomena, but has never been accustomed to the
systematic arrangement of phenomena observed.
The former mind will be able to demonstrate by
argument the truth of its opinions; but the latter
mind will be able to feel only, and not to demonstrate, the truth of its opinions. But it does not
follow that the opinions of a man who can by
words demonstrate them to be true, are more correct than the opinions of a man who only feels them
to be true; on the contrary, it is more than probable, that if the man who is not able to argue
has had more experience than the man who is
able, in disputed cases, the man who has the best
of the argument will have least truth on his side.
Truth or knowledge consists in the compounding
and recompounding of a vast number of sensations: that mind contains most truth or knowledge which has experienced the greatest number
and variety of sensations. A good arguer is one
who excels in the decompounding of the com-

pound sensations existing in his mind. A man of science is generally superior in argument to a man of art ; but a man of a certain art is in most cases superior to the man of the corresponding science in knowledge, or in the command of that subject which it is the common object of the art and science to attain. A man of art is able to state, with great certainty, what effect will follow certain causes ; but if the reasons for his opinions be demanded, he will find himself at a loss, and will be unable to render any reasons which may not be refuted by a man of science, far his inferior in knowledge.

Moral phenomena may be divided into two classes, one class containing those which relate more particularly to the faculties or powers of the mind, the other class containing those phenomena which concern most the affections of the mind, with regard to pleasure or pain. Phenomena of the first class will be presented in great abundance to the minds of such people as are accustomed to exercise themselves much in thinking on a variety of subjects. Phenomena of the second class will be presented in greatest abundance to those who are accustomed to the enjoyment of the greatest number and variety of pleasures and pains. The phenomena of the former class will be found in the greatest abundance and variety, in that nation which contains the greatest aggregate of knowledge on all subjects; the phenomena of the latter class will be most abundant and various in the nation which enjoys pleasures in the greatest number, intensity, and variety. But the knowledge of every subject is based on the phenomena most closely connected with that subject; the greater the number and variety of phenomena, the greater the knowledge, or the greater the approximation to truth. Hence, that nation which has the greatest aggregate of knowledge, will entertain the most correct opinions concerning the faculties or powers of the mind; and that nation which partakes of the greatest number and variety of pleasures, will know best in what things the mind receives most pleasure.

The knowledge of the powers of things and of mind, is, however, very intimately connected with the knowledge of the affections of the mind with relation to pleasure and pain. If men had no knowledge superior to that possessed by brutes, they could have no pleasures which are not common to the brutes. As knowledge increases, pleasures increase. The pleasures of brutes and of the lowest order of men amount to very little more than the cessation of pain; the pleasures of a well cultivated mind contain something of

a positive nature, by reason of the connexion
formed in the mind between many passions. A
brute or a man of the lowest order, will think
itself as happy as a man of cultivated mind. An
ignorant mind can form no conception of the
pleasures enjoyed by a cultivated mind: what
cannot be conceived, cannot be desired, consequently an ignorant mind cannot prefer the condition of a cultivated mind to that of its own.
A man born blind will not desire much the condition of men who have the sense of sight; he
will think himself to be as happy with his four
senses as other men can be with five senses.
The question whether a contented ignorant mind
be as happy as a contented cultivated mind, is a
question of the same nature as this,—whether
a contented man who never had more than four
senses is as happy as a contented man of five
senses? If this question be answered in the af-
firmative, then it follows as a necessary consequence, that the lowest order of animals, or those
animals which can hardly be said to have one
sense, are as happy as the highest order of men.
If this question be answered in the negative, then
it follows, that the greater the number of senses,
or the greater the number of inlets for pleasure
and pain, the greater is the absolute or aggregate quantity of pleasure enjoyed by a mind.

That is to say, the capacity of a mind for pleasure increases, as the number of passions in that mind are increased.

Every nation believes itself to be more happy than every other nation ; every people thinks its own institutions to be more conducive to happiness, than the institutions of any other people. Every Englishman believes himself to be happier than a Frenchman, and a Frenchman thinks himself happier than an Englishman. If England excelled France in all branches of knowledge, then the Englishman would be right, and the Frenchman wrong. Although the aggregate knowledge of the English nation be greater than the aggregate knowledge of the French nation ; yet it does not follow that the Englishman's opinions respecting happiness, will be more correct than those of the Frenchman. On the contrary, if the Frenchman has experienced a greater variety of pleasures than the Englishman, his opinions concerning happiness will undoubtedly be the most correct, which is certainly the case. The general knowledge of a Frenchman is so nearly equal to that of an Englishman, that they may be regarded as having equal experience in solitary mental pleasures. But in social pleasures of all kinds, the experience of the French is vastly superior to that of the English. Knowledge of any subject, is proportional to the number and variety of phenomena observed relating to that subject. Since, therefore, the phenomena relating to happiness are more numerous and varied in France than in England; the opinions in France about happiness are more true than the same kind of opinions current in England, and the French nation are happier than the English nation. France is more happy than England, not because it possesses a greater aggregate quantity of knowledge ; but because it possesses a greater quantity of that particular branch of knowledge which relates to pleasure, and at the same time is nearly equal to England, in the aggregate of all branches of knowledge.

If all opinions were free, it would always happen that the nation which excels all other nations in all classes of opinions but one given class, would also have excelled in this class of opinions. That is to say, the nation which possesses the greatest aggregate of knowledge, would also possess the greatest quantity of knowledge on any particular important subject. For instance, if opinions on happiness were free, England would excel all other nations on the subject of happiness as much as it does on every other important subject. In that case, knowledge would be happiness, and happiness would be proportional to knowledge : the

nation containing most knowledge would always
contain most happiness. The freedom of discus-
sion on the subject of pleasure or happiness, is
powerfully checked in England by two obstacles;
one of which is the proscription by national prejudices of all books which broach any new theory of
happiness; the other obstacle is, the great encouragement given by public funds and private
funds to the ingenious supporters of the current
favourite theories of happiness. The highest order of English minds, cannot publicly express
their opinions on the subject of happiness, because they would injure their private interests by
so doing. In consequence, the English common-
alty remain in ignorance of those subjects, which
it most concerns them to know. When the above
mentioned obstacles are removed, England will as
rapidly outstrip other nations in the knowledge of
happiness, as it has outstripped them in all other
branches of knowledge.

The greatest and most pernicious error into
which all the world have fallen, is, that happiness consists in money, wealth, or the command
of slaves. This error is greater, or is more deeply rooted in the minds of Englishmen, than in the
minds of any other people. This error, like all
other errors, arises from an induction founded on
too small a number and variety of phenomena.

The English are accustomed to the enjoyment of a smaller number and variety of pleasures than other nations; they are, consequently, more liable to the adoption of erroneous opinions on the subject of happiness. The possessor of much money or slaves is not at all happier than the possessor of a small quantity of money or slaves : the happiness of a man seldom or never increases with his income. Money or slaves can make no addition to the happiness of a man who has an abundance of the necessaries of life, and of the society of men and books. The belief that slaves or money is happiness, is manifestly the cause of a vast deal of misery to the suffering labourers and slaves; and this misery of the slaves does not occasion one particle of happiness to their masters. It has been beneficently ordained by providence that no man or classes of men can increase their happiness by oppressing, or by diminishing the happiness of other men or classes of men. The law of Nature is, that the interests of individuals and the interest of the public shall always be inseparably linked together.

That the love of money is the root of all evil, is one of the greatest truths. Nothing retards the progress of knowledge more than the love of money. If the half of the mental labour which has been expended in the world on the getting of money, had been expended in the acquisition of useful knowledge, the human race would at this time, have approached very near to perfection. The love of money becoming the ruling predominant passion of the mind, excludes all useful mental pursuits. There is another way by which the love of money checks the progress of knowledge; this is, by the effect it produces on the publicly expressed opinions of the men of cultivated understandings, whose opinions rule the opinions of all other men. Cultivated minds imbibe a passion for money, because, in the present corrupt state of things, the society of other cultivated minds cannot be enjoyed without money. This passion for money being formed, a well cultivated mind will present to the world *not* the opinions he sincerely entertains, but those opinions which will yield him most money. Opinions which are most in unison with the prejudices of the vulgar, or of the unthinking part of the community, always yield most money; and the opinions of the vulgar are almost always false. Thus the love of money arrays the majority of the men of talent against truth.

Happiness depends very much on power. A nation possessing little power, can enjoy very little happiness, because it will lie at the mercy of the surrounding more powerful nations. But power is almost always proportional to knowledge : the nation which has most knowledge will always be found to possess most power. Knowledge is power. Of two neighbouring nations, nearly equal in knowledge or power, the nation containing the lower aggregate of knowledge may possess a superior quantity of knowledge on one particular subject; as that of happiness. It will then probably happen that the nation having most knowledge will not have most happiness, if it allows the less powerful nation to be at peace with it. National happiness is proportional to the aggregate of knowledge, and to the knowledge of the particular subject of human happiness ; that is, national happiness is proportional to national power and knowledge of happiness. It may, however, be regarded as a general rule to which there are very few exceptions, that all moral and physical arts and sciences are improved unitedly, not separately, in all nations ; that is to say, no art or science can be improved in any nation, without all other arts and sciences in that nation being simultaneously equally improved. According to this general rule, knowledge would be always followed by power and happiness : and the nation which excels another in knowledge, would also excel it in power and in happiness.

Useful knowledge may be divided into two

parts, physical knowledge and mental knowledge. Useful physical knowledge, is that which has for its object the diminution of the labour required to provide a given quantity of the necessaries of life, as food, clothing, lodging, and national defence.   Useful moral or mental knowledge, is that which has for its object the knowledge of the faculties and affections of the mind, with the view of being applied to the improvement of physical knowledge, and to the increase of human happiness.   It is in this sense alone I would wish my readers to understand the term knowledge.   Every man as well as every other animal is in pursuit of happiness.   But man, through ignorance, very frequently renders himself miserable by the performance of certain actions, which he expected would lead him to happiness.   If man knew wherein happiness consisted, and if he knew what were the best means of attaining it, he could not fail to arrive at happiness; which is to say, *knowledge is happiness.*

BOOK THE FOURTH

BEING THE APPLICATION OF THE PRINCIPLES
CONTAINED IN THE PRECEDING BOOKS.

CHAPTER I.

Application to Nations in general.

BEFORE proceeding to the practical application
of the principles contained in the preceding part
of this work, I will present to my readers a general summary of the most important of these
principles.

All things which yield pleasure to man, are the
effect of labour. The things which yield bodily
pleasures, may be obtained by the labour of other
men : but the things which yield mental pleasures,
and the capacity for receiving mental pleasure,
can be acquired only by the labour, activity, or
exercise of the mind of the individual. Since
bodily pleasures cannot be enjoyed without some

kind of bodily exercise, it may be asserted with considerable truth, that pleasure and labour are inseparably connected together; that a man who has expended no labour, can receive no pleasure; and that the pleasure of that man is the greatest, who reaps no more nor less than the effect of his individual bodily or mental labour, or of an equal quantity of labour.

The prime necessary of life is food; the secondary necessaries of life are clothing, lodging, national defence, and knowledge. I call these latter necessaries secondary, because that, although man can exist without them, they are necessary for the distinguishing of the human race from the monkey race. Necessaries are the constituent parts of national and individual wealth, power, and happiness: the nation which possesses most food, clothing, lodging, national defence, and knowledge, is more wealthy, powerful, and happy than any other nation. A man's happiness is not affected by the quality of the food, clothing, or lodging, which he consumes. A man who has always been accustomed to live on vegetable food, derives as much pleasure from eating, as one who has been accustomed to live on animal food. A man who possesses clothing and lodging sufficient to preserve the body at its proper temperature, is as happy, in this respect, as a man clothed and lodged in the most sumptuous manner. The unhappiness which frequently attends plainness in food, clothing, and lodging, is not a consequence of the things themselves; but it is the effect of that pernicious vice found in the minds of most people, which is or may be called pride. If the erroneous passion or vice, called pride, were removed from the world,— that is, if men were not so foolish as to measure one another by their externals—then, a man enjoying the necessaries of life only, would be as happy as the man possessing the most splendid clothes, lodgings, equipage, and victuals.

The principle termed the " Division of Labour" is of the utmost importance. If men had always lived separate one from another, they could never have risen much above the level of monkeys. All the improvements of man originate in the collecting together of men in bodies. If there had been no division of labour, that is, if every man produced his own food, clothing, and lodging, the arts could have made little or no progress, and men could never have emerged from barbarism. As the ' division of labour' increases, the effect of a given quantity of labour increases. If, for example, in a certain stage of the division of labour, a man must labour four hours a day to provide himself with the necessaries of life; in a more advanced stage of the division of labour, he will be able to obtain the same necessaries, by labouring two hours a day. The effect of a given quantity of labour increases, as the number of men acting in concert increases. The greater the division of labour, the more rapid is the improvement, both in the arts and sciences.

Another important principle, which, like that of the division of labour, compels men to unite together in bodies, is Nature's law of gregariousness or sociality. Nature has so ordered it, that the majority of the pleasures of men are dependent on society. The happiness enjoyed by a man is, in most cases, proportional to the number and force of his friendships. The more numerous the society to which a man belongs, the more friendships will he have an opportunity of forming. Happiness increases as the number of men forming one society increases. Gregariousness also increases knowledge; for the actions of men towards one another, are moral phenomena; and the greater the society, the greater the number of phenomena, and consequently, the greater the knowledge of the moral arts and sciences. As the number of men forming one society increases, the saving of labour increases, happiness increases, and the rapidity of the progress made in the moral and physical arts and sciences increases.

The breed of men, like that of all other animals, is capable of indefinite improvement, in mind as well as in body. The bodies of a coming generation may be rendered superior in health, strength, and activity to the bodies of a present generation, by selecting for the purposes of propagation the individuals of both sexes possessing the most healthy, vigorous, and active bodies, and not suffering weak and diseased people to transmit their diseases and miseries to posterity. In a similar manner, the minds of a people may be improved by selecting for propagation those people who excel in the more useful qualities of mind, as justice, judgment, imagination, benevolence, &c.; and not permitting ideots or madmen, or people approaching to such, to propagate. The breed of men, like that of other animals, may be improved, not only by confining propagation to the best varieties of the species, but it may also be improved by the diligent and attentive culture of the minds and bodies of individuals taken indiscriminately. If the body of a child or other young animal, be carefully exercised until it arrives at maturity, it will be capable of producing much better bodies, as offspring, than it would if imprudently managed. The same is true of minds: a set of indifferent minds may, in a few generations, be converted into good powerful minds. A wise people will improve their bodies and minds, by the application of both of these laws of nature. The former law of nature may be very safely acted upon, for a population may be preserved stationary by means of the propagation of one half only of the females born, provided they begin to propagate at the age of puberty.

I shall now, by way of illustration, suppose the case of a certain number of colonists, who are about to settle in some distant isle, which is to be under no foreign dominion. The island I shall suppose to contain 5000 acres of land, and the number of colonists I shall suppose to be 1000, the women and children not being taken into account, although I am no advocate for the exclusion of women from governing. I will suppose all the colonists to be men of equal property, or that all of them have carried out stock of equal value, so that, on their arrival at the island, all will be regarded as possessing an equal right to the land, and an equal right to power. The colonists may be supposed to be taken indiscriminately from the population of their native civilized country; they will, in that case, have among them farmers, artificers, and scientific men. I shall suppose these colonists to be acquainted with the principles just now enunciated, and I shall show what line of action these principles will engage them to pursue. That the remarks in this chapter may not be deemed visionary and impracticable, I must observe, that the form of government recommended herein, is founded on the principles and doctrines inculcated in the Christian revelation, and every true Christian must give it his warmest support.

In the first place, the colonists, on their arrival at the island, will not divide the land into 1000 equal portions, and isolate each man on his five acres; for, in that case, the fruits of the " division of labour" could not be reaped, few or no social pleasures could be enjoyed, and every man's property and person would lie at the mercy of a stronger man or men. To escape the last of these evils, the colonists will league together for mutual defence from one another. Such a league is indispensable to the existence of every society; it may be termed a league for the enforcement of the claims of natural justice. The colonists will perceive that their whole body cannot, without much difficulty, be collected together, to investigate and pronounce their decision in every case of injustice which may occur. Moreover, they will perceive that, even if this could be easily effected, the decisions of such a large body would seldom be correct, by reason of the difficulty of communicating all the particulars to such a large multitude, and by reason of the inferior powers of judgment in the majority of this multitude. To remedy this inconvenience, the colonists will divide themselves into parties of ten each, and each party will select that man of their number whom they consider to possess the clearest discernment, and the most firmly rooted principles of justice. The men thus selected will be formed into a representative assembly of one hundred men. This assembly will find itself too unwieldy for the collecting of evidence, and the pronouncing of correct judgments, in the cases of ordinary and frequent occurrence; they will, in consequence, divide themselves into parties of tens, each of which will select its best man to represent it in an assembly of ten men. The administration of justice, in ordinary cases, will be entrusted to the assembly of ten. In trifling matters, or in matters of little importance, justice will be administered by a president, selected from and by the assembly of ten. In matters of the greatest moment, the administration of justice will be committed to the charge of the assembly of one hundred. These three bodies, the assembly of one hundred, the assembly of ten, and the president, will sometimes give their decisions separately, and sometimes collectively, according to the nature of the subjects for consideration. These three ruling bodies will be charged with the general government of the colonists, as well as the administration of justice between individuals. For the qualities of the mind which fit a man for the office of judge between individuals, are the same as those which render a man fit to discharge the office of judge between classes of men, and between conflicting opinions, for promoting the welfare of the public: these qualities are, as we have seen, a very clear discernment, and an ardent thirst for justice.

The colonists having thus secured what are called their rights of person and property, will, in the next place, direct their attention to the great saving of labour to be derived from the division of labour. All the men of the same trade will collect together in one mass, each man's machinery, stock, and labour, in other words, all the capitals of any one trade will be collected into one single capital. At least, one-half of the colonists will be agriculturists; the agricultural capital of the colonists, besides machinery and stock, will consist of the labour of five hundred men, or of the necessaries for the subsistence of five hundred men. Since all the agriculturists have an equal right to govern their collected capital, the government of this capital must be performed by an assembly of the whole number of agriculturists, or by their representatives. The difficulty of managing a capital, by collecting the opinions of five hundred men on every subject, would induce the agriculturists to select fifty of their most intelligent men as rulers of their capital. This assembly of fifty, finding it very troublesome to meet together on subjects of ordinary occurrence, will appoint an assembly of five, reserving to themselves the power of deciding on cases of more than ordinary importance. The general management of the agricultural capital will be entrusted to the assembly of five; cases of minor importance will be decided by a president chosen by and out of the assembly of five; cases of the greatest moment will be decided by the assembly of fifty. The goverments of the capitals in other trades will be regulated on the same principles as that of the agricultural capital. And the governments of all capitals will be subject to the general government.

The colonists may with advantage divide themselves into three principal classes or societies; viz. of agriculturists, of manufacturers, and of scientific men; these classes may be again divided into dependent classes. The men belonging to the scientific class would also belong to one of the other two classes, for the colonists would lay down this general law, that no man should be excused from the exercise of some bodily art or occupation; (bodily labour of some kind being necessary for health, and the labour in an art being conjoined with public as well as private utility.) The general government will determine the qualifications necessary for admission into the scientific class. The individuals governing the classes, and the individuals forming the general government, will receive no rewards for their labour of government; at least they will receive no other rewards than the mental pleasures which must arise from the consciousness of having performed their duty, and from being praised and respected by their fellow-citizens. These mental rewards are, however, far greater than any bodily or material rewards which it is in the power of a society to bestow.

After providing for the equal administration of natural justice, and after making regulations, by means of which the advantages arising from the " division of labour" may be attained, the next object of the colonists will be the increase of social pleasures, or the increase of gregariousness. This object may be best attained by the colonists dividing themselves into parties or families of ten each; the individuals forming a family being those who are most attached to one another by friendship; children and grown people would then be separated. Each family should have a separate sleeping apartment; a hundred of these apartments might form one house or building. The dining together in one common hall of four or five hundred people, and the having sitting rooms, lecture-rooms, libraries, &c. common to the whole population, will be sufficient for the gratification of the gregarious propensities of man. The colonists will then be united together by three bonds, viz. the equal administration of justice, the division of labour, and the love of gregariousness. The more perfect the administration of justice, the greater the division of labour, and the greater the gregariousness, the more closely will the whole of the population be linked together. When gregariousness, and consequently friendship, shall have increased in a very great degree, injustice will disappear; and people, instead of endeavouring to benefit themselves by injuring others, will endeavour to procure the good will of others, by the sacrifice of their own apparent interests. In such a state of things, the bonds of society would be two only, friendship and the division of labour. The equal administration of justice is, however, the base of the other two bonds of society; if the administration of justice be perfect, the division of labour and gregariousness cannot fail soon to arrive at perfection.

The above will be the general outline of the government formed by the colonists. I shall now notice some of the particular regulations which will be made by the colonists or by their general government. If the extent of the island admits of no increase of population, the general government will enquire of the scientific class, what number of births annually are necessary for the preservation of the population as its stationary number. The government will not allow the annual births to exceed this number, and they will not allow the sickly and weak in body or mind to propagate, to the exclusion of the healthy and vigorous in body or mind. A certain limited number of births will be required annually, and the government would act with great injustice to the present and future generations, if it took the births from the weaker part of the population instead of the stronger part. The education of the children will be chiefly committed to nature. Children will be suffered to rule and govern themselves by a representative assembly formed in the same way as the grown people's government. A system of the more useful bodily and mental exercises may, however, with advantage, be prepared for the use of such children as are willing to use it. Slight artificial encouragements or rewards may be proposed ; but pain should never be used as a stimulant. The love of excellence, or the love of power, is the chief stimulant used by nature; the introduction of any new stimulant will probably be productive of evil rather than good to the minds of children. The colonists will encourage public dancing and theatrical performances, for the benefit of the bodies of the present and rising generations; for the actions of players and dancers may be regarded as public lectures, on the graceful carriage of the body, addressed to the passion of imitation, which is the earliest and commonest of passions. Public musical performances will also be encouraged; in fact every thing productive of pleasure will be encouraged. As a punishment for crimes, hard labour will be found sufficient in all cases, the degree and the duration of the labour being proportioned to the degree of crime: the excessive labour of criminals properly applied, will diminish the necessary labour of the rest of the community.

What I have said of the colonists and their island, is applicable to every town and its circumjacent country; and every township might pursue with the greatest advantage the course I have marked out for the colonists. Every state or nation is made up of townships; national power is the collected power of many townships. We will suppose a spacious territory to be divided into one thousand townships, whose institutions are similar to those we have supposed existing among the colonists. The association of the thousand towns under one government, should be conducted on the same principles as that of the thousand colonists. The whole number of towns should be divided into sets of tens and hundreds; every town should choose its representative, and every ten of the neighbouring representatives should choose one to represent them in the national assembly of one hundred. The national government must be constantly sitting; and it would be difficult and unnecessarily expensive to keep one hundred men constantly collected together at a great distance from their homes. For this reason, the national assembly of one hundred will appoint an assembly of ten, which latter assembly will appoint a national president. The ordinary affairs of the nation will be managed by the assembly of ten; cases of minor importance will be dispatched by the president; cases of extraordinary importance will be decided by the national assembly of one hundred. The thousand towns may be called a nation; one hundred of which may form a department and ten a sub-department. The sub-department, may be governed by the ten representatives of towns in the private matters of the sub-departments; and the internal public policy of each department may be regulated by the hundred representatives of its towns, or by the assembly of ten appointed by this assembly of one hundred. The representatives of towns, sub-departments, and departments, will be frequently changed or re-elected; lest the governors should contract too strong a habit of commanding, and the people too strong a habit of obeying them, which might endanger the national liberties. There is, however, no great danger to be apprehended on this head, since none of the representatives will receive any salary, and since all the people will possess equal or nearly equal shares of property.

In the same manner as the national general government was formed, so ought the national government of each class to be formed. For instance, the class of agriculturists of every town should choose their representative, and every ten of these representatives should choose their representative, and so on. The classes of manufactures and of scientific men should proceed in the same manner; so that for every assembly which represents all classes united, there should be a corresponding assembly representing the class of agriculturists; a corresponding assembly representing the class of manufacturers, and so on for the different classes. By means of such a system, the best information will be condensed into the smallest compass, and the government will possess the fullest vigour and intelligence. The assemblies of one hundred will select their cleverest men to form assemblies of ten, and every assembly of ten will select their cleverest man to act as a general president. The decisions of the assemblies of ten will probably be as correct as those of the assemblies of one hundred, and the decisions of the presidents will be nearly as correct as those of the assemblies of ten; but small ruling bodies act with much greater energy and consistency than large ruling bodies. All classes united may be under the regulation of their wisest man, as national president; and each class may be under the regulation of the wisest of their profession, as president. In such a system a very close approximation may be made to truth, in a very short time, by the national president's collecting the opinions of the presidents of classes on any proposed subject.

The system which has just been explained may be denominated the *social system*, on account of its being based on gregariousness and equality. Under the social system no man will toil in the production of material luxuries for the enjoyment of another man; and no man will produce material luxuries for his own consumption, because he will be persuaded that the pleasures arising from bodily luxuries are insignificant, in comparison with the mental luxuries which may be purchased by a small quantity of mental labour. Under this system, a man will obtain the necessaries of life by means of such a quantity of labour as is necessary for the preservation of his bodily health ; the remainder and the greater portion of his time, will be expended in mental labour and enjoyments. The social system is the best of all systems, because it most closely imitates nature, because it unites men by the powerful bonds of self-interest and love, and because it most accelerates the progress of man in knowledge, power, and happiness. And lastly, the social system is the best, because it is the only one which can be reconciled with the plain unperverted doctrines of Christianity.

CHAPTER II.

Application to England in particular.

THE social system is the limit towards which all governments tend, and at which they cannot fail to arrive sooner or later. The power of foolish governors has frequently been set in array against the power of nature : some men have foolishly attempted to subvert the laws which nature has laid down for the progress of the human race to perfection. But in most cases, the efforts of such men have produced effects contrary to those intended ; instead of delaying, or preventing a certain crisis, they have generally accelerated the arrival of the dreaded crisis. It is extremely doubtful whether the improvement of mankind has been more delayed by bad rulers, or tyrants, than by those who were called good rulers. The progressive improvement of mankind, it is not in the power of man to prevent. A wise demoniacal ruler might, however, considerably delay the progress of knowledge among his subjects, but I doubt whether such a man can exist ; every man must love his own interest, and every wise ruler must perceive that his own interest is inseparably connected with the interests and knowledge of his subjects. If the progress of knowledge should happen to be much slower in one nation than another, this evil will soon be remedied by nature. The instrument by which nature has secured the universal diffusion of knowledge, is war, or the law of the strongest ; and nature invariably connects strength or power with knowledge. A conquering nation always communicates the whole, or part of its knowledge, to the conquered nation. The power of the nation which first adopts the social system, will so far exceed the power of other governments, that they will fall an easy conquest to it, and be compelled to adopt the same social system. The British nation is the one which, in all probability, will soonest arrive at the social system, and which will spread the social system over the whole world.

England is more powerful than any other nation, because its government approaches nearest to the social system. Gregariousness prevails to a very little extent in England, but the other two bonds of the social system, viz. the equal administration of justice, and the division of labour, exist in England in greater force than in any other nation. A perfect administration of justice cannot fail to produce a perfect division of labour,

which latter cannot fail to produce perfect or extreme gregariousness. The administration of justice is very far from perfect in England. The
English laws are probably the worst in the world,
because they are the most voluminous, and because they are the most expensive to the appli-
cant : if the laws alone were the guardians of
justice, there would be less of justice found in
England than in any other country. But public
opinion is the guardian of English justice : in
England justice is administered in spite of the
laws : no better engine of oppression and injustice
could be devised than this system of laws. The
rich and the unjust are prevented, in a considerable degree, from making use of these laws as
instruments of oppression, by the fear of having
the detestation of the public pointed against them
by the *press.* The heavy expense of justice, is an
insuperable obstacle to the poor man's obtaining
justice against the rich man, and is a great obstacle to the administration of justice between
equals in property. The heavy tax on justice, is
the greatest retarding force on England in her
progress to perfection.

The greater the freedom, and the greater the
security of property, the more rapidly will a nation advance to perfection. England may establish in a short time a very great degree of this

freedom and security of property by a very simple process. This process is the simplification and the diminution of the written laws, and the confiding of the administration of justice chiefly to those principles of justice which nature has implanted in the mind of every man living in a society. The people of each rank in a town should have justice administered to them by judges of their own choice and appointment; people of different ranks should have justice administered among one another, by judges taken from the ranks to which the conflicting parties belong. In order that property may be free, the tenure of all kinds of property must be rendered as simple as that of ready money. This simplicity might be very easily attained by a law to this effect—that no man's power over his property should extend farther than giving it or bequeathing it to whomsoever he pleases, as so much ready money, without any regulation or command over its subsequent disposal. If property were thus simplified and secured, England would quickly arrive at the summit of perfection in knowledge, power, and happiness.

The degradation of the minds of the labouring classes, is one of the principal vices in the English system. This degradation chiefly arises from the idle classes inculcating opinions which they know to be false on the minds of the labouring classes : for cultivated minds can make uncultivated minds believe what they please. The idle classes have not yet advanced far enough to discover that their interests are inseparably connected with those of the labouring classes, and that they injure their own interests by injuring the minds of the labouring classes. The chief injury is done to the labouring classes, by the praise lavished on marriage and propagation, and by the laws which encourage directly or indirectly marriage and propagation. If the labouring classes were left to themselves, they would probably never press against the bounds of subsistence, and pauperism would disappear from the land. The proper cure for pauperism is the effectual repeal of all the laws and institutions which stimulate marriage. The sudden repeal of the laws and institutions which stimulate marriage, would be very difficult. The safest and most expeditious way of repealing the greater part of these laws, &c., would be by the imposition of a tax on marriages : the obnoxious laws and institutions might thus be rendered a dead letter ; when the tax and the laws, &c., may be repealed at the same time.

The labouring classes should bear in mind these important truths, that their condition is not at all affected by high or low prices, by peace or war,

by public taxes or tithes, and that their condition is affected by nothing but the relation which
the supply of labourers bears to the demand.   If
the supply of labourers fall much short of the demand, the real wages of labour will be very high ;
if the supply much exceed the demand, the money
wages of labour will not represent even the necessaries of life.   The supply is furnished by the labourers themselves; they may contract the supply,
and consequently raise wages, by diminishing the
number of marriages and births, or by refraining
from marrying when wages are low.   The supply
of labourers might be so far diminished, that the
money wages of labour would represent nearly the
whole produce of that labour.   In England, the
money wages of labour does not represent more
than the third part of the produce of that labour ;
the remaining two-thirds is consumed by the
useless classes.   The labourers ought so to proportion the supply to the demand, *that by means
of labouring six hours a-day, they might obtain
such an amount of money wages, as would represent the necessaries of life, an assurance of fu-
turity, and a sufficiency of mental instruction
for themselves and children.*   If English labourers were to keep the supply a little within the
demand, they would receive more money as
wages only, than they are now accustomed to re-

ceive as wages and charity together. The money bestowed on charity is insignificant, compared with the money which labourers might get by keeping the supply of labourers below the demand. Every wise governor will encourage the elevation of the labouring classes; for if the labouring classes are far removed from want, there is very little danger of a national convulsion : most national convulsions have arisen from the misery, ignorance, oppression, and starvation of the labouring classes.

The well understanding of the nature and effects of taxation, is of the utmost importance to nations. There are, however, very few subjects of which the world is more ignorant than of taxation. A good system of taxation is one of the best instruments for the increase of the wealth or power of a nation ; but most systems of taxation hitherto practised, have impaired the power of the nation to which they have been applied. These erroneous systems have originated in ignorance of the constituent parts of national wealth or power, which are, plain food, clothing, and lodging, national'defence, and knowledge. All labour which is engaged in the production of these articles of wealth (which are the necessaries of life) is useful labour : all labour which is not engaged in the production of necessaries, is worse than useless, because it must be maintained by the wealth produced by the useful labourers. For the sake of simplicity, we may suppose the people of every nation to be divided into two classes only, useful and useless labourers. The proper object of taxation is to transfer labourers from the useless to the useful class. Most systems aim at increasing the labour employed in the arts of war ; no governors have yet perceived that the power of a nation may be most durably increased, by applying the produce of taxation to the increase of the labour employed in the arts of agriculture. In England, one-third only of the population are useful labourers ; the remaining two-thirds are useless labourers or idlers, who consume the wealth or necessaries produced by the useful labourers, without giving any thing in return. The proper object of taxation is, the increase of the proportion borne by the number of useful labourers to the whole population. This object may be attained by taxing all luxuries, and applying the money thus obtained to the maintenance of labour for the production of necessaries. England, like all other nations, applies the produce of its taxes to the maintenance of one kind of necessary labour only, that engaged in the arts of war. I will now offer a few observations on the best method of raising a given amount of taxes.

One of the greatest blemishes in the English

system of taxation, and of which the English nation, so intelligent in other respects, ought to be most ashamed, is the tax laid on knowledge. In order to increase one necessary they diminish another necessary ; to increase one sort of power they diminish another sort of power. The taxes on paper, books, pamphlets, &c. ought immediately to be removed; and the loss, if any, thereby sustained, may be made up by increasing the tax on some luxury. Articles of luxury, or bodily luxuries, are the only proper subjects of taxation; as long as these luxuries abound in a nation, there is abundance of food for indirect taxation. At the time of England's greatest warlike exertions, there was no perceptible diminution of these luxuries among the people, which is a proof that the exertions made by England were insignificant compared with the exertions she was capable of making ; the great increase of her labourers in the arts of war, created no perceptible diminution of her labourers on luxuries. The labour engaged in the production of some kinds of luxuries, is frequently indirectly useful; at least, in some degree : in a good system, those luxuries will be most heavily taxed which are productive of the least indirect utility. Luxuries may be divided into three classes, the first class containing those which encourage and improve agriculture ; the

second class, those which encourage useful manufactures, or the manufacture of necessaries ; the
third class, containing those which are productive
of no direct or indirect national utility.   The
luxuries of the third class ought to be most
heavily taxed ; in fact, no luxuries of the other
two classes ought to be taxed whilst any luxuries
of the third class remain.   The tax laid on luxuries of the second class ought to be ten times
heavier than the tax laid on luxuries of the first
class ; because agriculture is of ten times greater
national importance than manufactures.   But the
English system of taxation proceeds in diametri-
cal opposition to these principles.   Luxuries of
the first class are taxed more than cent. per cent. ;
luxuries of the second class are taxed about the
rate of twenty per cent. ; and luxuries of the
third class are not taxed above three or four per
cent.   The first class contains all liquors made at
home from nutritive grain, or roots.   The second
class comprehends fine clothes, satins, lace, &c. ;
wines, spirits, and other foreign luxurious productions, which are received in exchange for manufactures, together with the ships, &c. employed
in the interchange of luxuries.   The third class
contains, domestic servants, horses for pleasure,
costly furniture, and houses ; to which may be
added *butcher's meat.*

The whole of the English revenue might easily be raised by taxes on the third class of luxuries; if such were the case, the wealth and power of England would presently be vastly increased. The existing English system of taxation is probably the worst that could be devised ; it encourages the consumption of the most useless luxuries, and diminishes the consumption of less useless luxuries. Although the national power might undoubtedly be greatly increased by levying the taxes principally from luxuries of the third class, yet the adoption of such a plan ought not strongly to be insisted upon, because it violates the important general rule, that the best government is that which allows the greatest freedom in the disposal of property or income. The system of taxation most to be recommended, is that which equally taxes all articles of luxury, with whatever degree of indirect utility they may be attended. A tax levied in this way would be of the same nature as a direct property-tax, but the pain and difficulty attending direct taxation would be avoided. A tax of thirty per cent. on all articles of luxury, would be about the rate of tax required for the raising of the whole English revenue. It would not be necessary to tax all articles of luxury; the taxing of the principal articles consumed will be fully sufficient : the rate

of tax must, in that case, be a little higher than
it would have been if all articles of luxury were
taxed. These advantages would attend such a
mode of taxation, that the total national revenue
would be. affected by no other fluctuations than
those in the value of money; and that the national revenue may be increased to a certain given
amount, suddenly and precisely, by a certain increase in the rate of taxation, which may be
calculated. Suppose, for example, (as is probably
the case,) that 10*l.* represent the luxuries consumed annually by every individual in England.
If the revenue required for an ordinary year be
at the rate of 2*l.* each individual, this revenue
may be raised by a tax of twenty per cent. on
all luxuries. If the national revenue required for
an extraordinary year be at the rate of 2*l.* 10*s.*
each individual, this revenue may be obtained by
a tax of twenty-five per cent. on all luxuries; and
so on for any required revenue. But under the
existing system, it is impossible to calculate with
any tolerable degree of accuracy what will be the
amount of the revenue of the coming year, prices
remaining constant. For an individual who spends
in one year his 10*l.* in malt liquors or spirits, which
are taxed at the rate of one hundred per cent.,
may spend it in the next year on luxurious clothing, which is not taxed more than ten per cent.

He will, consequently, pay 5*l.* to the government one year, and only 1*l.* the following year. The produce of the English revenue, under the present system of taxation, is affected by every change of fashion. When fashion leads people to consume articles which are heavily taxed, the revenue increases; when it is the fashion to consume things lightly taxed, the revenue falls off.

There is one kind of tax which deserves a particular recommendation, since it would have the effect of increasing knowledge, power, and happiness, in a great degree. The kind of tax I allude to, is a tax for the encouragement of gregariousness or sociality. Under the present existing selfish system, every family separates itself as much as possible from every other family; every family occupies a separate house, cooks its own food, and burns a separate fire. The consequence is, than ten times as much labour and money as is necessary is expended in house-building and furniture, in coals, and in the dressing of food; besides, the loss of happiness is very great, by reason of the degree of solitariness inseparably connected with this unnatural system. The national loss of labour and happiness occasioned by this pernicious system, may be gradually diminished until the evil ·is entirely removed by a very simple tax. A certain tax should be im-

posed on every house and fire used by one family only ; a lower tax should be imposed on a
house and fire used by two families ; a still lower
tax on the house and fire used by three families ;
and so on. Such a tax would increase both private and public wealth or power.

The knowledge of the nature and effects of
money is of the utmost importance to mankind.
It is for want of a proper understanding of the
nature of money, that the world is in such a de-
plorable darkness on the subjects which most
concern the happiness of man. The most barbarous people are better acquainted with the
fundamental doctrines of political economy, than
the most civilized people. There is no barbarous
or savage nation which is not firmly convinced
that all the articles which satisfy the wants of the
body, such as food, clothing, lodging, &c., are the
effects of labour ; there is not a savage nation
which does not know, that population is always
pressing against the bounds of subsistence, and
that wars and famines are useful in the keeping
of the population within the limits of easy subsistence. Most civilized men are totally ignorant of
these important truths ; and of the few civilized
men who are acquainted with these truths, the
acquaintance is more verbal than real. Most
civilized men refer all commodities to money,

not to labour, as their cause ; they believe that
certain commodities are with difficulty attainable,
not because they cost much labour, but because
they cost much money; — they believe that individuals and nations are poor and weak, because they have got little money, *not* because
they have little spare labour ;—they believe that
men are prevented from marrying and propagating *not* through want of the means of subsistence
but through want of money. This vulgar error
is very easily accounted for, on the principles of
mental association which I have explained : commodities and money are perpetually présented by
nature to the mind in the relation of cause and
éffect ; money and labour are less frequently presented in conjunction than in disjunction, so that
there exists no connection in the mind between
money and labour,—it follows, therefore, that money will be looked upon as the first cause of commodities. The root of all political ignorance
among civilized men, is the firm connection established in their minds between money and commodities, in the inseparable connection of cause and
effect. Money has, however, no necessary connection with commodities ; labour can produce
commodities as well without as with the interven-
tion of money. It is a common vulgar pernicious
error, that there exists a necessary connection be-

tween money and some commodity of real value, or some commodity which has cost labour, as gold or silver. Nevertheless, a bit of paper, which costs an infinitely small quantity of labour, may perform all the functions, as money, of a large quantity of gold or silver.

A cheap and steady currency is of very great national importance. England may obtain a cheap currency by a very simple process, viz. by abolishing the use of gold and silver money, and using paper and copper money only. A cheap currency might be thus easily obtained; the method of preserving a steady currency is now to be considered. All commodities are the effects of labour, but a given quantity of any commodity will not be produced by the same quantity of labour in every country, or in the same country at different times. However, a given quantity of the chief of all commodities, viz. corn, is the effect of the same, or very nearly the same, quantity of labour in every country, at the same or different periods. In other words, (as I have elsewhere shown,) *a given quantity of corn is the universal measure of value.* By a steady paper currency, is to be understood one in which a paper counter or bank note of a given denomination always represents or nearly represents the same quantity of corn. In order to establish a

currency of this kind, the number of paper counters in circulation must remain constant or nearly
constant. If, at any time, a counter-exchange for
more than the stated given quantity of corn, the
number of counters must be increased ; if, on the
other hand, a counter represent in ordinary years,
less than the stated quantity of corn, the number
of counters in circulation must be diminished. In
order that prices and currency may be under well
regulated control, it is necessary that public companies alone should be empowered to coin or issue
paper-money counters. No merchants or other private individuals ought to be suffered to issue bills
of exchange, which have all the effect of paper-
money counters, and which, consequently, disturb
and render unmanageable the regular bank note
or paper counter currency. England might obtain a secure, cheap, and steady paper currency
in the following manner; — by establishing in
every township one banking company for the
issue of all the paper-money or counters current
in the township ; and by establishing a national
banking company for the coining of all the paper
counters, current between the townships, or necessary for the balancing of the commodities in-
terchanged by the different townships. The prices
of commodities would then be under the absolute control of the national banking company, if

every other banking company were compelled to give national bank notes in exchange for its own notes.

The art of agriculture is by far the most important of arts: national power can in no way be so much increased as by giving great encouragements to agriculture. I shall now offer some observations on the encouragements which the English national government may with the greatest advantage afford to agriculture. In the first place, for every town and its neighbourhood, there should be formed an agricultural committee, which should be chosen by the farmers and land-holders of the township; the members of this committee should receive a small salary. All the committees in a county should choose members for a county committee; and the county committees should appoint a national committee or board of agriculture. The government will consult the board of agriculture on the disposal of the sum of money it intends to confer as rewards for agricultural distinction. Rewards will be proposed, for the grain, roots, or grass produced of the most superior quality; for the greatest improvement in the breed of draught cattle; for the greatest improvement in the management of land; for the greatest improvement of agricultural machinery; and for the best treatise on different agricultural subjects.

The man who excels all the competitors of the
same township, will receive a lower reward than
the man who excels his competitors of the same
county ; and the national prize will be greater
than the correspondent county prize. The committees of the towns, counties, and nation, will be
appointed distributors of the prizes. The names
of the prizemen will be published and recorded
for the sake of an additional stimulus. The
government should bear the expense of an agricultural library for every town. Other useful arts
might receive encouragement in a similar manner,
with great advantage to the national wealth and
power.

The tithe system is the cause of much moral and
physical evil to England, and a better system
ought to be substituted. The progress of agriculture is very much retarded by the existing
method of levying tithes ; the taking of the
tenth-part of the produce, prevents the cultivation
of inferior lands, and the increased cultivation of
rich lands. The national power (which so much
depends on agriculture) would be much increased
by a legislative enactment,—that tithes should be
a certain fixed proportion to rent, as one-fourth
or one-fifth of the rent. In that case, tithes
would be in the same predicament as rent, and
would do no more injury to agriculture than rent

does. It has been stated, by the best authorities, that the rent of all the lands in England does not represent more than the fifth-part of the gross produce of the land. If tithes, therefore, were rigorously exacted, the tithe revenue of England would be equal to half of the land-rent revenue; and the English clergy would receive the third part of all direct revenue from land, or, what amounts to the same thing, the English clergy has a fair title to the third part of all the lands of the nation.

Lamentations, that misery is inseparable from the condition of man, are perpetually assailing our ears. That a vast deal of misery does exist in the world, is an indisputable fact. It has been my object to show, that misery is not inseparably connected with man, and that the causes of misery are to be found in the ignorance of men. I think it has been shown, to the satisfaction of every impartial reader, that all national and in-dividual misery may be traced up to those vicious practices, customs, or institutions, which violate, or incline men to violate, the Divine precept, DO UNTO OTHERS AS YOU WOULD THEY SHOULD DO UNTO YOU. I am well aware of the perti-nacity with which people adhere to their national prejudices; I am well aware that people regard their vicious customs, &c., as the cause of the small portion of happiness which they enjoy. These hurtful prejudices cannot be suddenly removed, without the infliction of severe pain, as in a surgical operation. Men cannot be suddenly cured of their misery without suffering a very painful mental operation, rather than submit to which, they will undergo the severest bodily pains. Men always resist the power which endeavours to substitute new correct notions, for their old false prejudices. The greater the force exerted to instil new notions, the greater is the force of resistance, or the greater is the pertinacity with which the old prejudices are adhered to. Hence the danger of exerting a great force in the uprooting of false popular prejudices; for if the force exerted should happen to be diminished or relaxed too soon, then will the tide of ancient false prejudices roll back the tide of new correct notions, and the ancient prejudices will be established more firmly than ever. The affording of every facility to the diffusion of knowledge, and the exerting of a slight force against popular prejudices, are the only means by which a people can be safely and securely improved. Of all changes, those are the most insecure which originate with the lower orders of the people. Even if such changes should be conformable to truth, or conducive to happiness, it would be impossible for ignorant minds to carry them into effect; the exceptions to the general truth would stagger them, they would reject the truth in despair, and things would return to a worse state than before. No other beneficial changes can be regarded as permanent, except those which proceed from the thinking part and the rich part of the community, which are the two classes to which the bulk of the community seldom refuse their respect and obedience. A good reforming government will do nothing with violence; it will avoid all shocks to the feelings or interests of classes or individuals; it will never resort to compulsion, before all the means of conciliation have been tried without effect. In a word, such a government will regulate its actions by that divine precept of universal application, " *do unto others as you would they should do unto you.*"

THE END.